Dead Sea Scrolls
The Complete Story

Dead Sea Scrolls
The Complete Story

DR. JONATHAN CAMPBELL

Ulysses Press 🕮 Berkeley, CA
1998

Published by: Ulysses Press
P.O. Box 3440
Berkeley, CA 94703-3440

ISBN: 1-56975-092-0

First published in the United Kingdom as *Deciphering the Dead Sea
Scrolls* by Fontana Press

Printed in Canada by Best Book Manufacturers

10 9 8 7 6 5 4 3 2

Cover Design: Big Fish

Library of Congress Cataloging-in-Publication Data
  Campbell, Jonathan G. (Jonathan Goodson), 1964-
    The Dead Sea scrolls : the complete story / Jonathan Campbell.
      p. cm.
    Includes bibliographical references and index.
    ISBN 1-56975-092-0 (alk. paper)
    1. Dead Sea scrolls—Criticism, interpretation, etc. 2. Qumran
  community. I. Title
  BM487.C36 1997
  296.1'55—dc21   97-37220
                                                              CIP

Distributed in the United States by Publishers Group West

For Beryl and Colin

On that day the deaf shall hear
the words of a scroll,
and out of their gloom and darkness
the eyes of the blind shall see

Isaiah 29:18

CONTENTS

LIST OF PLATES

Fragments of Tobit in Aramaic from Cave 4 (4QTob^{b}ar)

Fragments of Jubilees from Cave 4 (4QJub^d)

Fragments of sectarian work called Miqsat Ma'ase ha-Torah (4QMMT^d)

Scroll Jars discovered by Bedouin in Cave 1

Several columns or sections of the sectarian Habakkuk Commentary from Cave 1 (1QpHab)

Section of the longest Dead Sea Scroll called the Temple Scroll from Cave 11 (11QT^a)

Section of the long Isaiah Scroll from Cave 1 (1QIsa^a)

Westerly view towards Cave 4, from the edge of the outcrop on which lies Khirbet Qumran

A cistern at Khirbet Qumran, probably split by the earthquake of 31 BCE

Southerly view over the ruins of Khirbet Qumran

LIST OF MAPS AND DIAGRAMS

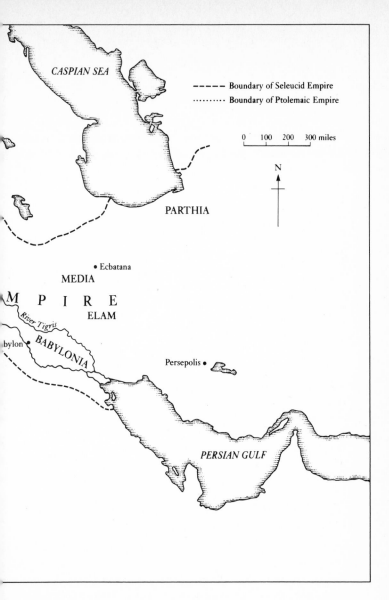

CASPIAN SEA

---- Boundary of Seleucid Empire
········ Boundary of Ptolemaic Empire

0   100   200   300 miles

N

PARTHIA

• Ecbatana

MEDIA

M   P   I   R   E

ELAM

River Tigris

bylon • BABYLONIA

Persepolis •

PERSIAN GULF

The Ptolemaic and Seleucid Empires

ACKNOWLEDGEMENTS

Several friends and colleagues supported me in the production of this book. Among them Mary Betley and Jason Reese deserve special thanks for the way they selflessly worked through early drafts of each chapter and provided me with feedback. I am equally grateful to Geza Vermes and Alison Salveson, who made numerous constructive observations at a later stage and helped me bring the project to completion. The eagle eye of proofreader Liz Cowen was also much appreciated. Last but not least, I would like to thank Philip Gwyn Jones and Toby Mundy at HarperCollins, whose patience and enthusiasm were invaluable in reaching our common goal.

J.C.   *July 1996*

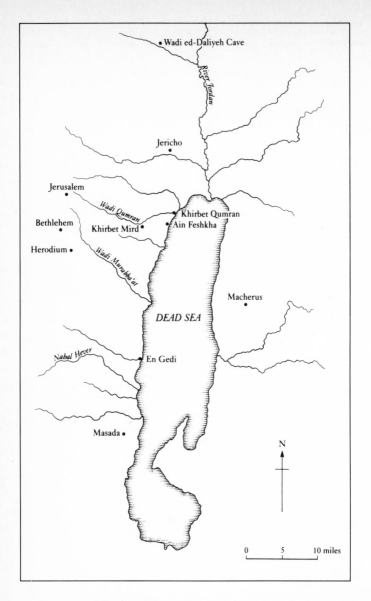

The Dead Sea and surrounding area

CHAPTER 1

What Are
the Dead Sea Scrolls?

SETTING THE SCENE

The Dead Sea Scrolls are the name given to a unique collection of ancient Jewish manuscripts written in Hebrew, Aramaic and Greek. Roughly two thousand years old, they were discovered quite by chance between 1947 and 1956 in eleven caves around a site called Khirbet Qumran on the north-western shore of the Dead Sea.[1] Many important texts were published early on, but it was only after the release of fresh material in late 1991 that most ordinary scholars gained unrestricted access to the whole corpus.

The aim of this book is to explain to the uninitiated in plain language the nature and significance of these amazing manuscripts. For nearly fifty years now, they have had a dramatic effect on the way experts reconstruct religion in ancient Palestine.[2] Cumulatively and subtly, the detailed evidence of the Dead Sea Scrolls (DSS) has gradually transformed scholars' understanding of the text of the Bible, Judaism in the time of Jesus, and the rise of Christianity. In the chapters to follow, therefore, each of these subjects will be looked at in turn, while Chapter 6 will deal with some of the more outlandish proposals made in recent years. First of all, it will be fruitful to clear the ground by defining exactly what the Dead Sea Scrolls are.

DISCOVERY OF THE CENTURY

The DSS have rightly been described as the most important archaeological find of the twentieth century. The best way to begin explaining why is to report how and when the contents of the caves around Qumran were found. The story has been recounted many times before, of course, and it is not always easy to disentangle the facts from legendary accretions that have grown up around the basic plot. Nevertheless, even though the numerous accounts that exist are difficult to harmonize in every detail, we can get a reasonably accurate overview of what took place from the recollections of several of the individuals involved.[3]

In early 1947, three young shepherds from the Ta'amireh Bedouin tribe were in the vicinity of the springs of Ain Feshkha. This site, some two miles south of Khirbet Qumran, sits on the narrow coastal plain that lies between the western shore of the Dead Sea and the cliffs marking the edge of the Judaean hills. The three were grazing their flocks on the patches of greenery which here and there break the barren monotony of both the plain and the hills. One evening, while searching for a lost animal, the shepherd known as Jum'a casually threw a stone into one of the hundreds of caves found among the surrounding cliffs and hills. An unexpected crashing noise emanated from it and because it was nearly dark the young men determined to investigate further the next day. In the morning, Muhammed edh-Dhib was the first to enter the cave and, in one of a number of stone jars, each about two feet in height, he found three manuscripts, two of them wrapped in linen cloth. The Bedouin carried their unusual booty to the tribe's main centre and, soon afterwards, brought the documents to the nearest town, Bethlehem, in the hope of selling them. Unsuccessful, they left them with a cobbler-cum-antiquities dealer called Khalil Eskander Shahin.

We now know that the cave where the scrolls were found – subsequently dubbed Cave 1 to distinguish it from other caves with manuscripts located in the area – is situated less than a mile north of Qumran and some nine miles south of Jericho. Four further scrolls were retrieved from it by the Bedouin and lodged with the same antiquities dealer. Shahin, however, was unsure of the age or value of the manuscripts now in his care. Because they looked as though they might be written in the Syriac language, he contacted the Metropolitan Athanasius Yeshue Samuel of St Mark's Syrian Orthodox Monastery in Jerusalem.[4] The Metropolitan decided to purchase four of the texts: a near-complete copy of the biblical book of Isaiah, some kind of previously unknown religious rule book, a similarly distinctive commentary on the biblical book of Habakkuk, and a badly preserved paraphrase of parts of Genesis. Impatient to learn more about the documents, especially how much they might be worth, he investigated several possible avenues of further inquiry. Eventually, the Metropolitan approached scholars at the American School of Oriental Research in Jerusalem. One of the staff there, John Trever, took photographs of three of the compositions which, it transpired, were written in Hebrew; not long afterwards, he and his colleagues published the results in two volumes.[5] The fourth scroll, containing an Aramaic paraphrase of Genesis, was difficult to unravel due to its decomposed state.[6] This problem was compounded by the way the document was originally manufactured, for all the lengthy DSS originally consisted of leather or papyrus strips sewn into a single piece and then rolled up into scroll form.[7]

Meanwhile, Professor E. L. Sukenik of the Hebrew University in Jerusalem had heard rumours of a manuscript discovery. Despite civil unrest over the United Nations resolution to partition Palestine (then under British control) into an Arab state and a Jewish state, he managed to buy the three other scrolls in late 1947 from Khalil Eskander Shahin. The three compositions were all in Hebrew and consisted of a collection of hitherto unattested hymns similar to the biblical Psalms, a dramatic work about a cosmic battle precipitating the end of the world, and a second, less well preserved, copy of the book of Isaiah. Sukenik quickly realized that the scrolls were very old and of momentous significance – he was, after all, an expert in ancient Jewish writing with a speciality in burial inscriptions from the first centuries BCE and CE. So widespread was his reputation that, soon after he had acquired his own documents, an intermediary sought his opinion on the four Cave 1 manuscripts belonging to the Metropolitan. Sukenik was allowed to examine them briefly, risking life and limb by venturing under difficult political circumstances from Jewish Jerusalem to Arab Bethlehem to collect them. But then, much to the professor's disappointment, the Metropolitan unexpectedly opted to submit the four scrolls to the expertise of Trever at the American School of Oriental Research, as we observed earlier. Sukenik, like Trever, published his material fairly rapidly.[8] And today, these seven substantial manuscripts from Cave 1 are in Israeli hands, housed in Jerusalem's specially built Shrine of the Book.[9]

Both the American scholars and Sukenik issued separate press releases in April 1948, describing their documents in brief. So it was that, almost a year after the shepherd had disturbed the jars in Cave 1, the world at large came to hear about the remarkable discoveries that had been made.[10] It took some time for the news to sink in, however. Even experienced scholars were initially reluctant to believe that ancient documents could have survived in the Judaean desert, for received wisdom held that the conditions were simply too harsh. Only when further excavations got under way, despite the ongoing political tensions in the region, was it possible to demonstrate conclusively just how old the DSS were.

When the British relinquished their mandate on Palestine, David Ben-Gurion immediately declared the establishment of an independent state of Israel on 14 May 1948. In the military struggle that ensued, the Jewish state took possession of the land that would have been allotted to it under the earlier partition plan. It also took West Jerusalem, while Jordan annexed East Jerusalem and the West Bank. It was within the latter's boundaries that military officials eventually determined the exact location of Cave 1 in early 1949. Anxious not to lose any more scrolls either to the black market or abroad, the Jordanian Government had authorized the Arab Legion to comb the area, and the site was found by Captain Philippe Lippens of the United Nations Armistice Observer Corps. The soldiers had had to carry out their laborious task without the aid of the Bedouin who, hoping to find other valuable manuscripts for themselves first, were reluctant to co-operate with the relevant authorities.

Once its identity had been established, two scholars set about thoroughly excavating Cave 1. They were G. Lankester Harding (director of the Department of Antiquities of Jordan) and Roland de Vaux (director of Jerusalem's famous Dominican college, L'Ecole Biblique et Archeologique de Jerusalem Française). In addition to the documents removed earlier, they retrieved various other artefacts, including pieces of text that had broken off several of the seven large manuscripts, as well as fragments of what were obviously the remains of other compositions. These fragments were published in the first volume of an official series with Oxford University Press called *Discoveries in the Judaean Desert*.[11] Then, in 1950, the antiquity of both the manuscripts and the fragments was dramatically confirmed, when the results of Carbon-14 tests on the linen wrappings from two of the scrolls gave a date of

33 CE.[12] Even allowing for the two-hundred-year margin of error inherent in carbon dating at the time, the ancient origin of the literary contents of Cave 1 was now beyond doubt.

Surprisingly, at this early stage it did not strike Harding and de Vaux that the manuscripts from Cave 1 might be linked to the nearby ruined buildings of Khirbet Qumran, perched just above the coastal plain on an outcrop from the cliffs overlooking the Dead Sea.[13] In fact, a preliminary survey led them to conclude it was unconnected to the scrolls. However, a fuller investigation took place in late 1951, and the archaeologists came to a different conclusion. The remains of a jar like those which had been found in Cave 1 were retrieved from the Qumran site and this important link, along with other common items, convinced them that both the cave and the ruins were related.

In the ongoing search for new caves and new texts, local Bedouin were at a distinct advantage. Although their interest was solely financial, their familiarity with the Judaean desert meant that they tended to be the first to discover literary deposits, which they would then sell to the archaeologists, who were working under the auspices of the Jordanian Government. In this way, the Jordanians were prepared to spend considerable sums of money to acquire scrolls from the Bedouin and, by preventing their entry into the black market, keep the documents under the Jordanian jurisdiction of the Palestine Archaeology Museum in East Jerusalem. Some of the manuscripts bought from the Bedouin turned out to have no direct connection with either Khirbet Qumran or Cave 1 – such as the finds in similar caves further south at Wadi Murabba'at and Nahal Hever (described at the end of this chapter). More positively, Cave 2 was discovered in 1952 and, over the next few years, several other sites were located – Caves 3, 4, 5 and 6. Their contents, like those of Cave 1, seemed to be linked with the ruined buildings at Qumran. Indeed, Cave 4 was situated right next to Khirbet Qumran and provided particularly rich literary pickings.

In view of the strong link with the caves, three further excavations of the ruins took place. During one of them, Caves 7, 8, 9 and 10 were discovered by the archaeologists, who then embarked on a final examination of the Qumran buildings in 1956. On the basis of coins and pottery, as well as distinct layers within the ruins themselves, the excavators concluded that Qumran had undergone two periods of habitation. In the seventh and eighth centuries BCE, a town had stood on the site – perhaps the City of Salt mentioned in the Bible at Joshua 15:62. Then, after a break of several centuries, the evidence pointed to a second occupation from some time after 150 BCE until 68 CE. Although the buildings could have provided up to two hundred people with communal facilities for eating, ritual bathing and worship, the group's members must have lived in the surrounding caves which, though bereft of manuscripts, contained other items linking them to Qumran. Life would certainly have been harsh in these conditions, for, at 1,300 feet below sea level, the Dead Sea region gets very hot and humid. However, it was possible to collect water in cisterns in the rainy season, while local springs such as Ain Feshkha would have allowed some farming. The remains of pottery kilns and tanning facilities provide further evidence that a subsistence lifestyle was indeed feasible in this hostile environment. As hinted already, moreover, those using Qumran during this second period also busied themselves copying and studying the manuscripts deposited in Caves 1–10.[14]

The last cave, Cave 11, was discovered by the Bedouin in early 1956. It contained several lengthy texts, including a collection of canonical and non-canonical psalms all ascribed to King David, an Aramaic paraphrase of the biblical book of

Job, as well as a copy of Leviticus written in Old Hebrew.[15] Because the Palestine Archaeology Museum was experiencing funding problems by this stage, these scrolls were entrusted for publication to Dutch and American scholars whose institutions put up the money to buy the documents from the Bedouin. As for the Temple Scroll, the longest of all the DSS at nearly 27 feet (over 8 metres), it was not acquired until 1967. As early as 1960, though, rumours were circulating that it had been hidden by Shahin, the antiquities dealer who had supplied Sukenik and the Metropolitan. The scholar-cum-politician Yigael Yadin therefore retrieved the document, with the help of Israeli military intelligence, during the Six-Day War of 1967, when Israel occupied East Jerusalem.[16] By then, the DSS were becoming symbolic of Israeli identity, providing a tangible link between the new state and the last time the Jewish people inhabited their own land two thousand years earlier. The fortress of Masada, which will feature later on, took on a similar status, representing Jewish perseverance through adversity during the Arab–Israeli wars of the 1950s, 60s and 70s.

SCROLLS IN ABUNDANCE

The results of archaeology and carbon dating soon showed that the DSS stemmed from the last two or three centuries BCE and the first century CE. Certainly, they had lain in the caves undisturbed for centuries. We shall see later on that the texts probably belonged to a religious community of Essenes which flourished at Qumran for nearly two hundred years. The group apparently disbanded in the late 60s CE when Roman legions marched past Qumran on their way to Jerusalem to quash what scholars call the First Revolt of the Jews against

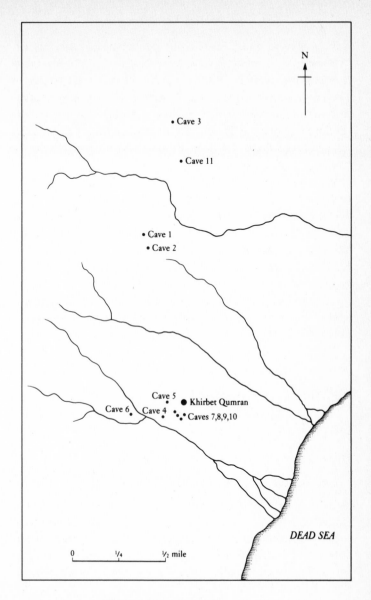

N

• Cave 3

• Cave 11

• Cave 1
• Cave 2

Cave 5
• Khirbet Qumran
Cave 6 • Cave 4
•••• Caves 7,8,9,10

DEAD SEA

0   ¼   ½ mile

Khirbet Qumran and Caves 1–11

Rome.[17] Fortunately for us, they left behind a collection of literature which is vast by any standards. It encompasses both complete manuscripts, like the lengthy Isaiah Scroll from Cave 1, as well as thousands of tiny fragments. Surprisingly, even such scraps often yield small amounts of legible text, as in the case of a commentary on the biblical book of Micah from Cave 1. In between these two extremes are many other manuscripts in varying states of repair.

With all these manuscripts, fragments and caves, it is easy to get confused. A system of letters and numbers has been devised, therefore, as a simple way of referring to individual documents from the DSS collection. Thus, the long Isaiah Scroll just mentioned is usually referred to as 1QIsa[a]. Here, 1 = Cave 1, Q = the site of Qumran, Isa is a standard abbreviation for the biblical book of Isaiah, and [a] = the particular copy (to distinguish it from 1QIsa[b], the other Isaiah text recovered from the same site). Acronyms of this sort have been apportioned to the all manuscripts found in Cave 1:

1QS — Community Rule (S = *serekh*, Hebrew for 'rule')

1QpHab — Commentary on Habakkuk (p = *pesher*, 'interpretation')

1QH — Hymns Scroll (H = *hodayot*, 'hymns')

1QM — War Scroll (M = *milchamah*, 'war')

1QapGen — Genesis Apocryphon ('ap' stands for apocryphon).[18]

Similarly, the fragments of a work from Cave 5 and Cave 6 known as the Damascus Document can be referred to as 5QD and 6QD, while the eight copies of the same composition from Cave 4 are called 4QD[a–h].

Alternatively, and easier still, a numerical system has been devised in which all but the seven major manuscripts retrieved from Cave 1 have been given numbers in sequence. According to this scheme, the commentary on Micah noted above may be designated simply as 1Q14, while 4QD^{a-h} can be dubbed 4Q266–273. Despite this procedure's straightforwardness, we shall opt to designate individual scrolls according to the lettered system whenever possible, because it often provides a clue to a document's contents.

Altogether, nearly eight hundred manuscripts were brought to light from the eleven caves. Cave 9 and Cave 10 yielded only one item each. At the opposite extreme, Cave 4 was the richest of all, providing scholars with over five hundred documents, some of them admittedly rather scrappy. To keep these numbers in perspective, it should be borne in mind that they include duplicate copies of the same work. The biblical book of Deuteronomy, for instance, was attested in no less than twenty-five manuscripts found variously in Caves 1, 2, 4, 5, 6 and 11. Taking such duplication into account, around four hundred distinct compositions have been preserved in all.[19]

To try and make sense of this mass of literature, it is helpful to divide the manuscripts into three basic categories. First, we have writings which were already known about before the DSS were discovered. In such cases, the main contribution of the finds has been to provide us with specimens which are much older than anything which had come to light beforehand. By way of illustration, we can turn to 1QIsa^{a} again, for it predates all other copies of the book of Isaiah in Hebrew by a thousand years. And scholars were delighted to find that nearly all the other scriptural books common to Jews and Christians turned up in the caves as well. To put it more concretely, thanks to the DSS, we now have specimens of biblical books which were actually being read by Jews when Herod the Great ruled Palestine (37–4 BCE), and when Jesus walked and preached in the Galilean hills (around 27 CE).[20] Alongside these biblical texts were several works from the so-called Apocrypha. This term was coined by St Jerome (*circa* 340–420 CE) to designate a number of books, like Tobit and Ecclesiasticus, which the Christians of his day regarded as part of the Old Testament, even though Jews by that time had excluded them from their Bible. Similarly, two fascinating books called 1 Enoch and Jubilees also belong to this first class of DSS material. Although they entered into neither the Jewish nor the mainstream Christian Bible, they had been preserved through the centuries before turning up at Qumran. In fact, they are part of a large body of non-biblical Jewish texts from the last few centuries BCE and the first few centuries CE which scholars dub the Pseudepigrapha. This term will be explained in the next chapter, when the overall significance of the first category of DSS material – biblical, apocryphal and pseudepigraphical literature – will be unpacked in more detail.

The second category of DSS texts differs from the first in that it consists of compositions which no one knew about before their chance discovery in the caves around Qumran. Like the first category, though, they were probably widely read in Palestine during the late Second Temple period. Only after 70 CE when Jews and Christians decided not to include them in their Bibles were they lost. An example here is the interpretative paraphrase of Genesis known as 1QapGen. Translating some of the biblical stories about Noah and Abraham into Aramaic, it fills gaps in the narrative along the way, often rather imaginatively. Since it refers to none of the distinctive practices and beliefs of the Essenes, however, it was probably in wide use, disappearing from the scene only once it had ceased to be copied by Jewish or Christian scribes after 70 CE. Alongside 1QapGen, the DSS have revealed a large number of similar works which, although scholars had previously been unaware of their existence, also circulated in Palestine during the last two centuries BCE and the first century CE.

By far the greatest sensation was caused by a third category of document among the DSS, also completely unknown before 1947.[21] This class contains writings which, in view of their content, must have been composed by the religious group that lived around Qumran. To distinguish them from all the other manuscripts, they are often referred to as the 'sectarian DSS', and they consist of a mixture of poetic and legal works, as well as pieces of Bible interpretation and narrative. We shall look at some of the most important sectarian documents in Chapter 3. For the moment, it is worth repeating that they almost certainly represent the beliefs and practices of a branch of the Essenes – one of several religious parties existing at the time, alongside the Pharisees and Sadducees. Before 1947, the only substantial information we had about them was contained in the second-hand accounts of two first-century CE Jews, Philo and Josephus, neither of whom were Essenes themselves. Now, to the delight of scholars, the sectarian DSS function as a unique window into the world of an actual community of Essenes. In fact, as the only surviving first-hand material from any Jewish group before 70 CE, their value is inestimable.

THE SCROLLS AND THEIR TIMES

Just where the value of the DSS lies will emerge as subsequent chapters unfold. Here, it will be a good idea to sketch their general historical background, for there is unanimous agreement about the period from which the texts sprang. More precisely, all serious scholars now relate the DSS to Palestine during the last two or three centuries BCE and the first century CE. However, it was not always so. Although right from the start Sukenik and Trever thought that the DSS were ancient, others disagreed. The main proponent of a medieval date, for instance, was the late American scholar Solomon Zeitlin who, right up to his death in 1976, maintained that the DSS were a forgery.[22] But, in reality, it became increasingly clear that they were ancient. Among the mounting evidence, we have already noted the results of carbon dating, coupled with archae-ological study of the Qumran ruins. Later on, we shall see that the allusions to people and events contained in the sectarian DSS further corroborate their antiquity.

The three centuries concerned, roughly 250 BCE to 70 CE, are part of what historians call the Second Temple period. This designation covers Jewish history from the rebuilding of the Temple in Jerusalem in the late 500s BCE until its destruction by the Romans in 70 CE. These six centuries, as many readers will realize, partly overlap with the biblical period, for the Old Testament – also called the Hebrew Bible or Hebrew Scriptures – deals with Israelite and Jewish history up to 400 BCE and beyond.[23] Obviously, such a vast time span is beyond the scope of an introductory study like this one. So, we shall focus almost exclusively on the last three hundred years of the Second Temple period in subsequent chapters.

Here, it is worth placing the Second Temple period in its broader historical context. Strictly speaking, it began around 515 BCE with the rebuilding of the Temple in Jerusalem on the site of the one that had been constructed in the tenth century during the reign of King Solomon.[24] Those responsible for its re-establishment were members of the tribe of Judah who had been given permission in 537 BCE to return to their homeland from exile in Babylon. By then, of the original twelve tribes of Israel, Judah was the only one left and, as such, it is not wrong to go on referring to its members as Israelites. More normally, they are called Judahites or, better still, 'Jews', while 'Judaism' designates their religion.

Unfortunately, the sources for the first half of the Second

Temple period are sparse. Nonetheless, on the basis of late Old Testament books and some other writings, it appears that the Jewish community was fairly autonomous. The Persian authorities were content to let them regulate their own affairs as long as they paid their taxes. This arrangement made sense, for, from the imperial point of view, the Jews lived in a far-flung and relatively unimportant corner of the Persian empire. Indeed, the small province of Yehud or Judah, as it was called, consisted only of Jerusalem and its immediate environs. As for the Jews themselves, life must have focused on the Temple in Jerusalem, as well as the High Priest and other officials who were in charge of the people at a day-to-day level. Central to their culture was the belief that God, although creator of the whole world, had a special relationship with the Jews in view of the covenant or agreement he had made with their ancestors long ago. The terms of that relationship were laid down in the Law of Moses (the biblical books of Genesis, Exodus, Leviticus, Numbers and Deuteronomy). This Law or Torah contained the guidelines for regulating the community, ostensibly in the form of a divine revelation given to Moses centuries earlier on Mount Sinai. A range of other scriptural books also began to circulate during this period in the form in which we would still recognize them today – Joshua, Judges, 1–2 Samuel, 1–2 Kings, Isaiah, Jeremiah, Ezekiel, the Twelve Minor Prophets, and the Psalms.

With the conquest of Judah by Alexander the Great in 333 BCE, things started to change. Greek language and culture, in particular, began to permeate Jewish society. At first, it was only on the margins but, by the second century BCE, the question of whether or not to adopt Greek ways was causing serious strife within Jewish society. Many pious Jews did not want to assimilate and, with the outright persecution of Judaism by the foreign king Antiochus IV, a rebellion erupted in 167 BCE. It was led by the Maccabee brothers. Under their successors, the

Hasmoneans, Judah – or Judaea, as it was called in Greek – expanded and broke away as an independent Jewish state between 141 and 63 BCE.

Notwithstanding this reassertion of traditional identity, the Jews remained divided. In particular, various religious parties came into being from the middle of the second century BCE, including the Pharisees, Sadducees and Essenes. These groups vied with each other for the attention of the Jewish masses, offering them alternative interpretations of Judaism for the age in which they lived. This complex state of affairs continued after the Romans took control of the area in 63 BCE. In fact, discontent increased under their rule, especially in the first century CE. Emperor Caligula (37–41 CE) did not help matters when, in search of divine honours, he decreed from Rome in 40 CE that a statue of himself was to be erected within the Jerusalem Temple. The turmoil that would have been sure to accompany such sacrilege was only averted by Caligula's timely death in early 41 CE.[25] The Roman administration on hand in Palestine, however, was little better. The ineptitude of a succession of Roman governors merely aggravated Jewish exasperation, particularly during the 50s and 60s CE. Eventually, armed revolt broke out against Rome in 66 CE, but, almost inevitably, the superior strength of the occupying Roman forces proved decisive. The revolt was quashed in 70 CE and culminated in the destruction of the Jerusalem Temple, thereby bringing the Second Temple period to a close.

The above account is only a brief overview of the Second Temple period; we shall have an opportunity to unpack it further in Chapter 3. Hopefully, enough has been said to show that the six centuries concerned had a unique history and identity, especially during the last three hundred years. In other words, Judaism in Second Temple times was distinct both from what preceded and what followed. As implied already, the exile of the sixth century BCE and the destruction of the Temple in

70 CE constituted turning points of momentous historical and religious significance.

Second Temple Judaism should therefore not be viewed as simply a continuation of the religion of Israel which had existed before the sixth-century exile to Babylon. To help maintain this distinction, in fact, experts usually refer to the latter as the religion of Israel, in order to differentiate it from the Judaism of the Jews after 515 BCE. Although many Jewish and Christian readers of the Bible today would not be familiar with this distinction, there can be no doubt that the exile caused the religious traditions of Israel to undergo substantial transformation. For example, it is almost certain that the Torah did not exist before the exile in the form in which it circulated afterwards – even though Jews in Second Temple times came to believe that it had been revealed to Moses on Mount Sinai. Likewise, it is highly likely that, contrary to the perception of Second Temple Jews, many Israelites before the exile were not strict monotheists; only in the Second Temple period did monotheism emerge as one of Judaism's distinguishing traits.

In a similar way, it would be wrong to assume that Judaism as it developed after 70 CE was a straightforward continuation of what had gone before. In reality, the loss of the Temple and priesthood required Jewish religion to change in important respects over several centuries. This process included the publication of the Mishnah (200 CE) and, later still, culminated in the compilation of the Talmud (550 CE). Both writings place obedience to the Torah at the heart of Judaism. Of course, Jews had kept to the Law of Moses before 70 CE, but that had been only one element in their religious culture. Now, the Torah became the very essence of Judaism. For the Jews of the Mishnah and the Talmud, moreover, the Torah did not simply denote the Pentateuch. It also came to include what is dubbed the Oral Torah – interpretations of and additions to the Law which, it was believed, had also been revealed to

Moses on Mount Sinai. This distinctive belief is characteristic of Judaism after 70 CE, but was not a major feature of Jewish religion in Second Temple times.

Second Temple Judaism, then, was not the same as the religion of Israel or Judaism as it evolved after 70 CE. The distinctions involved here may at first seem a little perplexing to modern Jews and Christians, not least because religious authorities prefer to emphasize elements of continuity. Such elements are real enough – before and after the exile, for example, the Temple was important, while prior to 70 CE and afterwards the Law played a vital role. Nevertheless, only by highlighting discontinuity and change can we appreciate the distinctive nature of Judaism in Second Temple times, especially during the last three hundred years, as well as the full significance of the DSS within their proper context.

CONSPIRACY OR COMPLACENCY?

At the start of this chapter, we noted that it is only in the last few years that all interested scholars have been given free access to the whole DSS collection. At first, this might seem a little incongruous, for we saw that the manuscripts from Cave 1 were all published in the 1950s, while the contents of the so-called 'minor caves' (Caves 2–3 and Caves 5–10) appeared in 1962.[26] In contrast, relatively little of the material from Cave 4 was published between the early 1950s and the end of the 1980s. Such a delay seems lax, to say the least. Indeed, back in 1973, after nearly twenty-five years of waiting, Professor Geza Vermes of Oxford University rightly described the situation as 'the academic scandal *par excellence* of the twentieth century'.[27] Nevertheless, there are no grounds for accusing the Vatican of a conspiracy to withhold Cave 4 texts which might have been construed as damaging to Judaism or Christianity. Claims along these lines made in recent years are sensationalist nonsense and we shall deal with them in our final chapter.

The real causes of the delay in publishing the Cave 4 material are disappointingly mundane. With hindsight, three principal reasons for this 'scandal' stand out. First, there has long been a tradition of 'finders keepers' within the world of archaeology. In other words, it is usually assumed that, when texts are discovered, they are the sole property of the excavators concerned until official publication has taken place. This way of thinking explains the reluctance of those entrusted with the Cave 4 documents to share their work with anyone outside the team. Unlike Trever and Sukenik, their insistence on producing definitive studies of every single scrap in their care slowed down the process by many years.

Second, in retrospect, the vast amount of material disgorged by Cave 4 was simply too much for the small team put in charge of the thousands of fragments – some of them no bigger than a postage stamp. Back in 1952, Roland de Vaux was made editor-in-chief of all the finds in the Judaean desert. He was assisted initially by three colleagues from the Ecole Biblique – M. Baillet, P. Benoit and J. T. Milik – who worked with him in the Palestine Archaeology Museum. But when the sheer quantity of Cave 4 texts became apparent, de Vaux decided to draw on a wider band of international scholars. In the decades that followed, J. M. Allegro, F. M. Cross, C. H. Hunzinger, P. W. Skehan, and J. Strugnell were each given a portion of manuscripts to work on. Even this enlarged body of academics, however, was not up to the enormity of the task.

Just why this was so is explained by a third impediment: most of the team's members had other jobs at the same time as they were working on the DSS. We may well imagine that their initial enthusiasm waned as the years rolled on and, not surprisingly, the first volume of Cave 4 material did not appear until 1968. Even then, it received bad reviews from other scholars for its sloppiness and inaccuracy, and a further nine years elapsed before a second volume was completed.[28]

During the Six-Day War of 1967, Israel seized control of the West Bank and East Jerusalem from Jordan. Automatically, jurisdiction over the Qumran region and over the Palestine Archaeology Museum – renamed the Rockefeller Museum – fell into Israeli hands. Sensitive to any external criticism, however, the Israeli Antiquities Authority decided not to interfere with existing arrangements for the publication of the DSS. As a result, the status quo under de Vaux continued. Even when P. Benoit succeeded him as leader of the team in 1971, he was no more successful in expediting progress.[29] The same applies to John Strugnell, who, taking the reins in 1987, increased the editorial team to twenty. But, as Vermes recalls, when he met Strugnell at a DSS conference in London that same year and asked for the photographic plates of the remaining Cave 4 material, his request was flatly refused.[30]

Things only began to improve significantly in 1990 when the Israeli Antiquities Authority accepted Strugnell's resignation after an Israeli newspaper reported that he had made uncomplimentary remarks about Judaism.[31] Strugnell was replaced by Emanuel Tov, Professor of Biblical Studies at the Hebrew University of Jerusalem and the first Jewish scholar to be put in charge of the DSS. Although he continued to restrict access to those approved by the editorial team, he reallocated the unpublished DSS among a much larger body of scholars – over fifty-five in total. Goaded by ongoing pressure from Hershel Shanks, editor of the widely read *Biblical Archaeology Review*, this alone would probably have speeded up the process of publication to an acceptable rate.

Yet the situation soon changed beyond all recognition. In 1991, two scholars issued a computer-based reconstruction of seventeen unpublished manuscripts from Cave 4.[32] They had used as a basis a copy of Strugnell's Preliminary Concordance, a list of key words in the DSS, issued privately in only twenty-five copies in 1988. Then, the Huntington Library of San Marino, California, one of several institutions that had a complete photographic set of all the DSS for safekeeping, announced it would allow scholars working in the field access to them. At first, the Israeli Antiquities Authority tried to oppose this development, but by the autumn of 1991 it was fighting a losing battle. As a result, all restrictions were lifted. Any scholar with a legitimate interest was allowed to view the photographs at Huntington, as well as the duplicate collections stored at the Ancient Biblical Manuscript Center in Claremont, California, in Hebrew Union College, Cincinnati, and in the Oxford Centre for Hebrew and Jewish Studies. In November of the same year, an edition of the photographs was published in book form – although it is not clear how the editors managed to prepare their photographic material so quickly.[33] There is now available a microfiche edition of all the DSS, prepared under the auspices of the Israeli Antiquities Authority itself, while the production of a CD-ROM version is also under way.

As a result of these dramatic changes, publication of those DSS from Cave 4 which had been kept under lock and key for over forty years has moved apace since 1991.[34] Included among them are important biblical manuscripts, in addition to sectarian works such as the text known as 4QMMT[a–f] or Miqsat Ma'ase ha-Torah (Some Precepts of the Law). Most scholars outside the editorial team had hitherto only heard rumours about the contents of such documents – although a few had been circulating semi-secretly at conferences or between individuals. In Chapter 3, we shall return to the impact of these new sectarian compositions, while Chapter 2 will examine the impact of the DSS on the Bible.

COMPETING DISCOVERIES IN THE JUDAEAN DESERT

Hopefully, it will be clear by now what the DSS are, at least in a basic sense. Before moving on, it is worth mentioning four other collections of ancient manuscripts which have been discovered in the same geographical vicinity. Indeed, over many centuries the Judaean desert to the west of the Dead Sea was a safe haven for all kinds of religious zealots and political refugees. Its sparsely populated and inhospitable environment provided the sort of peace and quiet conducive to religious experience, while the wilderness allowed dissidents who required anonymity to remain elusive to the authorities.

Despite the geographical connection, however, we can safely say that these other collections of texts, important as they are, do not link up directly with the DSS we have just described. The first corpus to mention is a body of literature found in a cave in the Wadi ed-Daliyeh region, some nine miles north of Jericho.[35] The documents, which are written in Aramaic and date from around 375 to 335 BCE, are mostly of a legal nature. They were the property of nobles from the city of Samaria who, recently conquered by Alexander the Great's army, had to flee after unsuccessfully rebelling against their new overlords in 331 BCE. The rebels were pursued and starved to death under siege in the cave where their remains were found by archaeologists in the early 1960s.[36] Although fascinating in their own right, these writings from Wadi ed-Daliyeh are obviously distinct from those found at Qumran.

A second collection comes from the impressive fortress of Masada, south of Qumran, originally built by the Hasmoneans. It was also home to some of the rebels of the First Revolt against Rome until 74 CE and, not surprisingly, a number of texts from that occupation were found by excavators between 1963 and 1965.[37] Among them was a small fragment of a work, identical to one found in Cave 4 at Qumran and known as 4QShirShab or Shirot 'Olat ha-Shabbat (Songs of the Sabbath Sacrifice). This has led some to suggest that, when the Qumran community abandoned its settlement in 68 CE, a proportion joined the rebels at Masada, only to be defeated with them in 74 CE. But this is pure speculation and we do not really know why a copy of 4QShirShab was attested at both Qumran and Masada.

Thirdly, numerous documents in Hebrew, Aramaic and Greek were found in caves around Wadi Murabba'at and Nahal Hever during the same period that the discoveries at Qumran were being made. Apart from the remains of biblical books, the most important texts relate to the Second Revolt of the Jews against Rome which took place between 132 and 135 CE. The leader of that uprising, a man called Simeon ben Kosba, is mentioned by name. Nevertheless, these documents clearly post-date even the youngest manuscripts from the Qumran caves, although some have been published in the series *Discoveries in the Judaean Desert*.[38] Like the material from Wadi ed-Daliyeh, however, a number of them can be precisely dated. Accordingly, a comparison of the texts from both Wadi ed-Daliyeh and Murabba'at with those of Qumran has allowed scholars to work out a general picture of the way Jewish writing developed between the fourth century BCE and the end of the first century CE. The technical term for this kind of academic research is palaeography.[39]

Fourthly and finally, a cache of texts in Greek, Syriac and Arabic was retrieved from a place called Khirbet Mird, midway between Bethlehem and Qumran, during 1952 and 1953. The site turned out to be a ruined Christian monastery founded in 492 CE. As such, the documents uncovered are all Christian, dating from no earlier than the fifth century CE. Obviously, they have no connection with the Qumran finds.

All four of these collections of literature from the Dead Sea vicinity have sometimes been dubbed DSS in view of their geographical origin. Fortunately, this is now less common than it used to be and, as should be clear by now, they do not relate directly to the contents of the eleven caves found around the site of Qumran. Without further ado, therefore, let us return to the DSS proper and look at their impact on our understanding of the Bible.

CHAPTER 2

The Dead Sea Scrolls
and the Bible

WHICH BIBLE?

The aim of this chapter is to explain what the DSS tell us about the state of the Bible in the last two or three centuries BCE and the first century CE. As we shall see, the biblical text in circulation was less fixed than modern Jews and Christians are used to, while the 'canon' or official list of books deemed to be scripture was more open-ended. For many readers, the subject under discussion will be a new one and, understandably, a little daunting. A few words on the Bible in the vernacular are in order here, therefore, to lay the ground for what follows.

Most people encounter the Bible through a translation in their own language, usually in the form of a Christian Bible containing both the Old Testament and the New Testament. As far as the English language is concerned, the first major translations were produced by John Wycliffe (*circa* 1330–84) and William Tyndale (*circa* 1494–1536), two Englishmen whose work was not always to the liking of the Church authorities. Tyndale, in fact, was strangled and burnt at the stake in 1536 for producing a vernacular rendering of the sacred text of the Bible, hitherto available in the Western Church only in its approved Latin version. Nevertheless, by the end of the sixteenth century, the Geneva Bible of 1560 and the Bishop's

Bible of 1568 were popular English versions with official sanction. Both were overtaken by another translation, however, produced under the authority of James VI of Scotland who ascended the throne of England as James I in 1603. Among Anglicans and Protestants, this Bible, the so-called Authorized or King James Version (KJV) of 1611, dominated the English-speaking world for nearly three hundred years, although the Roman Catholic Church produced its own English Rheims-Douai Bible in 1609–10.

By around 1870, it had become clear that the KJV had many defects. As a result, the Church of England commissioned a team of fifty scholars to work on a revision. It appeared as the Revised Version (RV) of 1885, with a sister translation in the United States of America called the American Standard Version. It had been intended that these efforts would result in definitive British and American versions, but in fact their publication merely marked the beginning of a long line of English-language Bibles offered to the public over the past one hundred years. Several were produced by individuals frustrated with the archaic language of versions like the RV.[1] Others were put together by translation panels whose members had to sign up to one set of theological convictions or another – thereby calling into question the objectivity of the enterprise.[2] A parallel example fashioned by a single person is K. N. Taylor's *Living Bible* of 1971 which, though admittedly a paraphrase rather than a translation, is riddled with inaccuracies inspired in part by the work's prior commitment to a Protestant fundamentalist position. Quite ludicrously, for instance, Taylor renders 1 Kings 14:24's condemnation of the 'male temple prostitutes in the land', where the Hebrew *qadesh* (literally 'consecrated man') specifically denotes sacred ritual prostitution, as 'there was homosexuality throughout the land'. Turning to a New Testament example, the *Living Bible* simply omits the problematic reference in John 12:14 which states that Jesus himself, rather than the two disciples mentioned in Mark 11:2, found the donkey he rode into Jerusalem.

Fortunately, four good English renderings of the Bible have appeared in the last decade or so, each a revision of an earlier one. The first to mention is the New Revised Standard Version (NRSV) of 1989. This constituted a revision of the Revised Standard Version (RSV) of 1952 and was sponsored by the National Council of the Churches of Christ in the United States of America. Although the language of the NRSV is modern throughout, the translators chose to follow in the tradition of the KJV, RV and RSV. In other words, they tried to be 'as literal as possible and as free as necessary' in their rendering of the original Hebrew and Aramaic of the Old Testament, and Greek in the case of the New Testament.

In contrast, the Revised English Bible (REB) is a looser translation. It was produced in 1989 by a team of scholars who were supported by nearly all the Christian Churches of Britain and Ireland. Following in the footsteps of its radical pre-decessor, the New English Bible of 1970, the REB rejected the concern of the KJV–RV–RSV tradition for literalness in favour of an equally accurate but more idiomatic English rendering. Just as fresh in its approach is the New Jerusalem Bible, published in 1985. It was a revision of the Jerusalem Bible of 1966, based on the work of Roman Catholic scholars from the Ecole Biblique in Jerusalem – an institution which featured in the last chapter. Finally, *Tanakh: the Holy Scriptures* was produced by the Jewish Publication Society of America, also in 1985. It is in use among English-speaking Jews all around the world; obviously, it does not include the New Testament.

All four of these translations of the Bible have been produced by competent teams of scholars. Naturally, they have targeted Jewish and Christian readers who have neither the time nor the skills to read the Bible in its original languages. It should be stressed that each editorial team adopted a strictly objective approach to its task. The purpose, in short, was to offer the public a version which would accurately translate the underlying Hebrew, Aramaic or Greek texts in terms which the original writers intended. Such a commitment requires, for instance, that passages in the Old Testament, famous among Christians for the way they have been applied to Jesus, should be translated solely in relation to what they meant within ancient Israel centuries earlier. Although commissioned by explicitly Jewish or Christian institutions, therefore, readers can be sure that versions like the NRSV or REB constitute reliable, as well as readable, renderings of the scriptures into English.

Despite their common commitment to accuracy, a closer look will show that some noticeable differences exist even between trustworthy translations such as those described above. For the moment, it is worth explaining two types of divergence. The first has already been hinted at and is more apparent than real. At base, it is simply a matter of the style of language preferred by a given editorial team. For example, the scholars behind NRSV and REB have chosen to translate exactly the same underlying Hebrew words in Numbers 22:28 somewhat differently:

NRSV	REB
Then the LORD opened the mouth of the donkey, and it said to Balaam, 'What have I done to you, that you have struck me these three times?'	The LORD then made the donkey speak, and she said to Balaam, 'What have I done? This is the third time you have beaten me.'

In this example, the NRSV has a fairly literal, although perfectly understandable, translation. The REB, on the other hand, has tried to be more upbeat, preferring language that sounds more natural to most modern English users. In neither case is the meaning of the verse in dispute.

The second sort of divergence is of greater significance and reflects points where the underlying words of a given biblical verse are either ambiguous or problematic. In such cases, the various translation teams have sometimes opted for quite different ways of handling the text. Numbers 22:32 provides a suitable illustration:

NRSV	REB
The angel of the LORD said to him, 'Why have you struck your donkey these three times? I have come out as an adversary, because your way is perverse before me.'	The angel said to him, 'What do you mean by beating your donkey three times like this? I came out to bar your way, but you made straight for me . . .'

In this passage, the sense of the Hebrew of the final phrase is unclear and so the experts behind the NRSV and the REB have plumped for alternative solutions.[3] To put it another way, the two sets of scholars differed as to the most likely meaning of the last few words of Numbers 22:32, although both would doubtless agree that certainty is impossible in such cases. In these circumstances, modern English Bibles often fall back on footnotes to alert the reader to alternative ways of understanding the text. This can include appeal to biblical manuscripts among the DSS, but, as we shall see presently, they often raise as many new problems as they solve.

BIBLICAL STUDIES AND THE DEAD SEA SCROLLS

Some readers may be disconcerted by the example just given, for, contrary to popular belief, the words on the page of the Bible are not entirely fixed. Fortunately, the difficulties involved do not usually affect the basic meaning of a given passage. But there are exceptions. And, as we shall learn, even the list or canon of books contained in the Bible varies from one religious tradition to another – depending on whether the Bible concerned is Jewish, Roman Catholic or Orthodox, or Protestant.

In many other respects, university scholars working in the field of Biblical Studies – historical and literary analysis of the Old and New Testaments – have shown that the Bible is a less black-and-white affair than is often supposed. In the case of the New Testament, for instance, it would be generally recognized that the Gospels cannot be taken as strict historical accounts of what Jesus said and did.[4] On the contrary, many of the traditions about his life and ministry had undergone considerable embellishment by the time they were incorporated into the final edition of the Gospels during the last thirty years of the first century CE.

Turning to the Old Testament, also called the Hebrew Scriptures or Hebrew Bible, much has been learned about ancient Israel and early Judaism up to 400 BCE and beyond. For example, it now seems clear that many of the stories about the people of Israel in, say, Joshua or 1–2 Kings are idealized presentations. In other words, the narratives are not so much concerned with objective history as with teaching theological lessons about the relationship between God and Israel. What is more, Israelite practice and belief altered over the centuries and, as in our own day, rivalry between traditionalists and liberals seems to have been intense at certain times.[5] These and other insights have shown that the religion of the Old Testament was not some monolithic edifice but underwent periods of turmoil and change; as mooted in the last chapter, the exile of the sixth-century BCE was a particularly important watershed.

Due to this kind of work on the Bible over the past century, many individual books of the Old Testament have been re-dated. Study of the Pentateuch and Isaiah, for instance, has produced a re-evaluation of their age and origin. The results have understandably upset some Jews and Christians, especially around the turn of the century. By then, tradition had long held that Moses had written the Torah sometime in the second half of the second millennium BCE (1500–1000 BCE). Like-wise, the great eighth-century prophet Isaiah of Jerusalem was assumed to be the figure behind all sixty-six chapters of the book bearing his name. From the late nineteenth century, how-ever, scholars began to overturn many traditional notions like these. They concluded that the Pentateuch was actually com-piled in the sixth or fifth century BCE from several disparate sources. As for the book of Isaiah, only parts of Isaiah 1–39 truly reflect the ministry of the eighth-century prophet, while both Isaiah 40–55 and Isaiah 56–66 represent the work of anonymous figures working several centuries later.[6]

In fact, there is a wealth of internal data supporting the thesis that most Old Testament books were composed between 550 and 300 BCE after a long process of growth.[7] It would be tedious to go into too much detail, but a few illustrations may help. Numerous turns of phrase in the Pentateuch, for instance, could only have been penned after the time of Moses, while various repetitions or contradictions point to a long and com-plex editorial history rather than authorship by a single indi-vidual.[8] With the book of Isaiah, the vocabulary and imagery of chapters 40–55, unlike much of Isaiah 1–39, assume an audience already experiencing the exile of the mid-500s BCE

– not life in Judah during the eighth century.[9] Given the force of such observations, the need to re-date these and other Old Testament books is today accepted by all serious biblical scholars.

Nevertheless, some early commentators wondered whether the biblical DSS might provide fresh support for more traditional dates. It was pointed out, for example, that the community at Qumran treated the Pentateuch as a unit derived from Moses. Similarly, the fact that 1QIsa^a contains all sixty-six chapters of Isaiah in one long manuscript might suggest that the whole book derived from the prophet of the eighth century BCE after all. But there was a fatal flaw in the logic of such arguments. Although much older than anything available before 1947, even the biblical DSS are not sufficiently ancient to provide direct evidence for the state of individual books of the Bible during the period under dispute (*circa* 550–300 BCE). To do so, they would have to be several centuries older than they actually are. Returning to our concrete examples again, only if 1QIsa^a stemmed from around 550 BCE could it be used to reaffirm a traditional date of authorship, proving that all sixty-six chapters already existed as a fixed entity during the exile of the sixth century BCE. Likewise, it would take copies of the Pentateuch from 600 BCE or, preferably, earlier still to reaffirm a traditional date and thereby counteract modern scholarly theories.

In reality, 1QIsa^a was probably copied around 125 BCE, while the oldest Pentateuchal text from Qumran is 4QExod^f from *circa* 250 BCE. The most such biblical manuscripts demonstrate is that, by the third or second century BCE, Jews had come to associate a sixty-six chapter collection with the eighth-century prophet Isaiah. They had also come to view Exodus, along with the rest of the Torah, as emanating from the time of Moses. Yet, it has never been in dispute that nearly all the books of the Old Testament were in circulation by 300 BCE and that Jews soon afterwards developed traditions about the origins of their holy books – traditions which have persisted until relatively recent times. It is no great surprise to find both these factors confirmed by the DSS, stemming as they do from the last few centuries BCE. The relevant manuscripts among the collection are not old enough, however, to provide access to the previous stage in the development of biblical books.

That being the case, it makes sense to follow the main conclusions of academic study of the Bible during the past hundred years. All serious scholars, although disagreeing over details, would accept that most Old Testament books underwent a long period of growth, reaching their final edition, as stated earlier, between roughly 550 and 300 BCE. This judgement is based on clues which can be gleaned from meticulous study of the Bible, as we saw in relation to the Pentateuch and Isaiah 40–55. The biblical DSS do not alter this impression. Nowadays, increasing numbers within both the Synagogue and Church would accept these sorts of conclusions, while only conservative Jews and Christians, with a prior commitment to a fixed theological position, would feel obliged to reject them.[10]

THE BIBLE BEFORE 1947

Despite the negative conclusion reached above, we should not forget that the DSS have provided scholars with specimens of biblical books up to one thousand years older than anything previously to hand. This alone renders the DSS among the most significant archaeological discoveries of modern times, for they are of immense value in teaching us about the state of the biblical text in the last two or three centuries BCE and the first century CE. To appreciate the extent of their contribution, it will be helpful to assess the evidence available before the DSS were found. Essentially, there were three primary versions of the biblical text that could be drawn upon before 1947: the Masoretic Text, the Septuagint, and the Samaritan Pentateuch.[11] We shall say a few words about each in turn.

The traditional Jewish Bible as transmitted by the synagogue over the centuries is usually referred to as the Masoretic Text – or MT for short. The name comes from the Hebrew word *masorah*, meaning 'tradition', while the Jewish scholars who gave it its definitive shape in the eighth to tenth centuries CE are known as the Masoretes. The MT is written in Hebrew, the original language of all the books of the Old Testament – except for one verse at Jeremiah 10:11 and a few chapters in Ezra and Daniel which are in Aramaic. Now, when Hebrew and Aramaic are in use as living languages, as in biblical times or in modern Israel, they are written down solely by means of consonants. This feature may seem odd to those familiar with English or French, but it is quite normal for Semitic languages like Hebrew and Aramaic.[12] The MT, therefore, consists essentially of consonants only. For Jews in the Middle Ages, however, Hebrew was a sacred tongue and not in everyday use. Although the consonants of the biblical text had been stable for centuries, its lack of vowels laid it open to occasional mispronunciation and misinterpretation. It was here that the ingenuity of the Masoretes came in, for they incorporated a system of vowels into the text, placed above and below the main line of consonants, and thereby guaranteed both its pronunciation and interpretation. This improvement meant that older, vowel-less copies of biblical books were discarded. None, unfortunately, have survived, and so the oldest complete Bible belonging to the MT tradition is the so-called Leningrad Codex of 1008 CE, with Masoretic vowels intact. The first printed edition of the MT was published in Venice in 1524–5 and remains the basis of the modern Jewish Bible.[13]

The second source for the text of the Old Testament before 1947 was an old Greek translation of the Hebrew Scriptures called the Septuagint or LXX. According to a first-century BCE work called the Letter of Aristeas, an Egyptian king called Ptolemy II Philadelphus (283–246 BCE) decreed that a Greek translation of the Jewish Law should be prepared for his library in Alexandria.[14] Seventy-two Jewish scholars were brought to Egypt from Judaea to fulfil this task, although some parallel accounts envisage only seventy translators – hence the name Septuagint (or LXX) from the Latin word for seventy. According to the Letter, they carried out their work with the miraculous help of God, thereby guaranteeing its accuracy. While such details show that the account is partly legendary, it is likely that a Greek rendering of the Hebrew Scriptures was prepared in Egypt in the last two centuries BCE. A sizeable Jewish community certainly grew up in Alexandria during this time and most of its members were Greek-speaking. A Greek translation was readily available by the first century CE, moreover, for it is regularly quoted by the writers of the New Testament. With the spread of Christianity in the first and second centuries CE, the LXX became the standard Old Testament for the Greek-speaking Church. As a result, the oldest surviving specimens of the LXX are Christian copies from the third and fourth centuries CE.[15] Although that leaves a gap of several hundred years from the original translation, these ancient manuscripts of the LXX take us further back in time than the oldest copies of the MT which, as observed above, stem from the Middle Ages.

The third source for the text of the Old Testament before 1947 was the Samaritan Pentateuch, preserved over the centuries by the Samaritan community. The Samaritans broke away from Judaism at some uncertain point in time during the

Second Temple period, one of its main distinguishing features being a preference for a temple on Mount Gerizim near Shechem rather than that on Mount Zion in Jerusalem. As its name implies, the Samaritan Pentateuch contains only the five books of the Torah, for the rest of the Old Testament possessed by Jews and Christians is not accepted. As for the text of the Samaritan Pentateuch itself, it is now extant only in medieval copies and is written in what scholars call Old Hebrew or Palaeo-Hebrew.[16] This script, which was the regular form of Hebrew employed in Israel before the exile, continued in use among the Samaritans, whereas the Jewish community in Second Temple times replaced Old Hebrew with the precisely equivalent letters of the Aramaic script. So thorough was this replacement that it has remained in force to the present day. In fact, what were originally Aramaic letters are now considered the standard Hebrew script – sometimes called Square Hebrew to distinguish it from Old Hebrew.

Most of the time, these three versions of the text of the Hebrew Scriptures say the same thing. Taking all the books of the Old Testament as a whole, nonetheless, there are literally thousands of divergences between the MT and the LXX, as well as between the MT and Samaritan Pentateuch. The majority are of a minor nature. They concern the presence or absence of the definite article ('the'), or variations in the spelling of proper names, or else differences in number. By the time of the flood recounted in Genesis 6–9, for instance, the MT assumes that the world had been in existence for 1,656 years, while the LXX presupposes 2,242 years.[17]

More substantial disagreements also exist, although scribal carelessness rather than deliberate alteration often seems to have been the cause. Detailed examination can sometimes show what has happened, as a comparison of Genesis 4:8 in the MT and LXX, adapted from the NRSV, makes clear:

MT	LXX
Cain said to his brother Abel.	Cain said to his brother Abel, 'Let us go out to the field.' And when they were in the field, Cain rose up against his brother Abel, and killed him.
And when they were in the field, Cain rose up against his brother Abel, and killed him.	

The LXX here contains a straightforward rendering of the MT. Presumably, the original translators had in front of them a Hebrew text which was the same as the MT still in the possession of the synagogue centuries later. Yet, as the parallel arrangement highlights, there is one major discrepancy: the words 'Let us go out to the field' are absent from the MT. Because this phrase is required to complete the sense of 'And Cain said to his brother', it must have dropped out of the MT accidentally in the course of transmission. Hence, the LXX reflects a better form of Genesis 4:8, based on a purer version of the Hebrew in circulation before the omission took place. Most modern English Bibles quite rightly follow the LXX at this point, rather than the defective MT.

Elsewhere, discrepant readings are not so easy to sort out. Amos 3:9 in the MT, for example, refers to the coastal town of 'Ashdod', while the LXX talks of the vast empire called 'Assyria'. Because the words 'Ashdod' and 'Assyria' look almost identical in Hebrew, a tired scribe presumably misread one word for the other somewhere down the line of transmission – although we can no longer tell which way round this took place. Such ambiguity explains why the NRSV has 'Ashdod' in Amos 3:9, while the New Jerusalem Bible prefers 'Assyria'. There is no substantial problem here, though, for the overall message of Amos 3 remains unaffected, whichever option is taken.

In other instances, however, the import of divergences is more significant. The whole book of Jeremiah is a good case in point. In the LXX, it is about one-eighth shorter than the MT and arranged in a different order. This level of disagreement can hardly be accidental, as Jeremiah 10:3–11, adapted from the NRSV, illustrates:

> [3]For the customs of the peoples are false: a tree from the forest is cut down, and worked with an ax by the hands of an artisan; [4]people deck it with silver and gold; they fasten it with hammer and nails so that it cannot move. [5]Their idols are like scarecrows in a cucumber field, and they cannot speak; they have to be carried, for they cannot walk. Do not be afraid of them, for they cannot do evil, nor is it in them to do good. [6]*There is none like you, O LORD; you are great, and your name is great in might.* [7]*Who would not fear you, O King of the nations? For that is your due; among all the wise ones of the nations and in all their kingdoms there is none like you.* [8]*They are both stupid and foolish; the instruction given by idols is no better than wood!* [9]Beaten silver is brought from Tarshish, and gold from Uphaz. They are the work of the artisan and of the hands of the goldsmith; their clothing is blue and purple; they are all the product of skilled workers. [10]*But the LORD is the true God; he is the living God and the everlasting King. At his wrath the earth quakes, and the nations cannot endure his indignation.* [11]Thus shall you say to them: The gods who did not make the heavens and the earth shall perish from the earth and from under the heavens.

In this arrangement, the italicized text appears in the MT, but is missing from the LXX. Faced with such a glaring example of disagreement, an obvious question is which version represents the original? The likeliest candidate might seem to be the Hebrew of the MT, for the original language of Jeremiah was undoubtedly Hebrew. Why should the LXX be so different? Was the translator incompetent? Did he arbitrarily decide to omit several verses? Or, is it possible that the Hebrew he was translating, though now lost, was substantially different from the MT preserved by the synagogue?

Before the discovery of the DSS in 1947, scholars had little to go on to answer such questions, for the precise origins of the MT, LXX and Samaritan Pentateuch were lost in the mists of time. Normally they tended to prefer the MT. After all, the books of the Old Testament had originally been written in Hebrew or Aramaic, and Jewish scribes were renowned for their accuracy. Mistakes of one sort or another had crept in, as always happens when a text is reproduced from one generation to the next by hand, and, in such cases, it made sense to appeal to the LXX or the Samaritan Pentateuch. The LXX, in particular, often helped, as we saw in relation to Genesis 4:8. As for the Samaritan Pentateuch, it has usually been treated with more caution, for some of its distinctive readings reflect the ideological split between the Samaritans and the Jews.[18]

This approach to the relative merits of the MT, LXX and Samaritan Pentateuch still acts as the point of departure for most modern translations of the Old Testament. Some such guiding principle is attractive to scholars engaged in the practicalities of translation, for any concrete edition of the Bible requires a starting point. The four English versions commended earlier, for example, all take the MT as their point of departure for Jeremiah. Quite sensibly, on the other hand, when it comes to individual textual difficulties, such as that in Genesis 4:8, it is not unusual for the LXX to be followed.

Nevertheless, work done in recent years may suggest that the priority accorded to the MT can no longer be sustained.

When the biblical DSS are added to the MT–LXX–Samaritan Pentateuch equation they further accentuate the complexity of an already complex situation. We shall now explain why this is so.

The Qumran caves have yielded copies of biblical books which are much older than scholars had ever dreamt was possible. Over two hundred out of the eight hundred or so manuscripts recovered from the caves are biblical works and, although some found in Caves 4 and 7 are in Greek translation, most are written in Hebrew or Aramaic, the original languages of all of them. The sheer number of manuscripts, however, as well as the scrappy nature of some, makes grasping the significance of the biblical DSS no easy task. So, first of all, it is worth getting an overview of the documents.

Given the centrality of the Torah in Judaism, it is not surprising that books from the Pentateuch predominate, as can be seen from the following table:[19]

Biblical Book	No. of Copies	Biblical Book	No. of Copies
Genesis	15	Psalms	36
Exodus	17	Proverbs	2
Leviticus	13	Job	4
Numbers	8	Song of Songs	4
Deuteronomy	29	Ruth	4
Joshua	2	Lamentations	4

Judges	3	Ecclesiastes	3
1, 2 Samuel	4	Esther	0
1, 2 Kings	3	Daniel	8
Isaiah	21	Ezra	1
Jeremiah	6	Nehemiah	0
Ezekiel	6	1, 2 Chronicles	1
The Twelve Minor Prophets	8		

Deuteronomy, Isaiah and Psalms stand out from this list as of prime significance and, as it happens, they are the most frequently cited biblical books in the sectarian DSS. Although these figures suffice as a general guide, we should resist reading too much into them in view of the impact the harsh conditions of the Judaean desert can have on written documents. Some of the badly damaged manuscripts, assumed to be the remains of biblical books, for instance, might in fact be other compositions in which only scriptural citations survived. The absence of Esther and Nehemiah may similarly imply no more than that the Qumran community's copies had simply disintegrated by the time the DSS were found in 1947. Given the overall size and variety of the Qumran library, this seems the safest assumption, especially since every other Old Testament book, as well as a lot more besides, showed up in the Qumran caves.

What, then, do the DSS teach us about the state of the biblical text in the last three hundred years of the Second Temple period? More particularly, do they have any bearing on the reliability of the MT, LXX and Samaritan Pentateuch described above? There are two essential points to be gleaned from the data supplied by the manuscripts. Let us look at each of them in turn, before considering some more general lessons to be learned in their wake.[20]

The first seems reassuring, at least initially, because the biblical DSS confirm that the MT is an ancient tradition carefully preserved by Jewish scribes over the centuries. 1QIsaᵃ acts as a good illustration, for it is very close to medieval copies of the same book. Here and there, of course, there are discrepancies – as is only to be expected when over one thousand years of copying by hand lie between two specimen documents. The well-known acclamation of Isaiah 6:3 ('Holy, holy, holy is the LORD God almighty'), for example, is slightly shorter in 1QIsaᵃ than in the MT. Elsewhere, the Qumran copy seems to have a superior reading, as in Isaiah 49:25. The MT of this verse contains the awkward phrase 'captives of a righteous person'. 1QIsaᵃ, however, reads 'captives of a tyrant' and, because this fits better into the surrounding context, it has been adopted by the NRSV.

Occasionally, the biblical DSS furnish us with more striking cases of the same kind of correction. A good example concerns 1 Samuel 10:26–11:4. In the NRSV, this passage reads as follows:

[26]Saul also went to his home at Gibeah, and with him went warriors whose hearts God had touched. [27]But some worthless fellows said, 'How can this man save us?' They despised him and brought him no present. But he held his peace.

Now Nahash, king of the Ammonites, had been grievously oppressing the Gadites and the Reubenites. He would gouge out the right eye of each of them and would not grant Israel a deliverer. No one was left of the Israelites across the Jordan whose right eye Nahash, king of the Ammonites, had not gouged out. But there were seven thousand men who had escaped from the Ammonites and had entered Jabesh-Gilead.

About a month later, [1]Nahash the Ammonite went

up and besieged Jabesh-Gilead; and all the men of Jabesh said to Nahash, 'Make a treaty with us and we will serve you.' [2]But Nahash the Ammonite said to them, 'On this condition I will make a treaty with you, namely that I gouge out everyone's right eye, and thus put disgrace upon all Israel.' [3]The elders of Jabesh said to him, 'Give us seven days' respite that we may send messengers through all the territory of Israel. Then, if there is no one to save us, we will give ourselves up to you.' [4]When the messengers came to Gibeah of Saul, they reported the matter in the hearing of the people; and all the people wept aloud.

The words put into italics here for emphasis are present neither in the MT nor in the LXX. However, they are found in 4QSam^a, the remains of a copy of 1–2 Samuel from Cave 4. Because the extra words improve the flow of the story, the editors of the NRSV included them in their translation. That was a sensible decision. Indeed, the fact that 'But he held his peace' and 'About a month later' look very similar in Hebrew almost certainly caused a scribe's eye to pass over the intervening words accidentally at an early stage in the narrative's transmission. Such a slip would explain why the words are absent from the MT and LXX, while Josephus, writing in the first century CE, knew about the details they contain when he wrote his own history of biblical Israel.[21]

The evidence presented so far might be taken to confirm the priority of the MT. But there is another side to the coin, for our second principal deduction from the biblical DSS is that other forms of the biblical text were in circulation during the Second Temple period alongside the MT. More precisely, diverse editions of biblical books were recovered from the Qumran caves. 1QIsa^a, for instance, does not seem quite so near to the MT when set alongside 1QIsa^b, which is virtually identical to it. And, while many other biblical DSS also closely resemble the MT, some variously reflect the text of the LXX or that of the Samaritan Pentateuch. 5QDeut, in fact, contains readings paralleled by all three versions – the MT, LXX and Samaritan. Still others exhibit new readings unknown before the discovery of the DSS.

The implications of this kind of divergence can be highlighted by turning once more to Jeremiah. Earlier, we noted that the MT and LXX represent substantially different editions of the book. When the remains of five copies of Jeremiah turned up in Cave 4, the assumption was that either the longer (MT) or shorter (LXX) version would be shown to have priority. As it happens, the bearing of 4QJer^{a-e} on the issue is not quite what was expected. On the one hand, most of the Jeremiah manuscripts from Cave 4 are close to the MT, confirming its antiquity. However, 4QJer^b contains the remains of a Hebrew version of the shorter text of Jeremiah as evidenced in the LXX. Its existence proves that, in the case of Jeremiah at least, the translator of the LXX was not incompetent, nor did he deliberately alter his text. Rather, he used an alternative Hebrew edition of the book which must have been circulating alongside a longer one during the Second Temple period.

Taken together, these two main features of the biblical DSS have led to a gradual transformation of the way scholars view the text of the Old Testament in recent decades. Not only does the textual tradition represented by the MT go back to Second Temple times, but so do the traditions reflected in the LXX. Indeed, all but a handful of the Samaritan Pentateuch's distinctive readings now seem to be merely general variations, devoid of any special Samaritan significance. Clearly, therefore, many biblical books existed in more than one version during the last two or three centuries BCE and the first century CE. Such diverse editions existed side by side in the Qumran caves and, since there is nothing specifically sectarian about the variations, we may presume the same situation prevailed outside the community as well.

Put this way, the evidence of the DSS challenges what most scholars have assumed for much of the past century. It used to seem sensible to think that the divergences evident in a comparison of the MT, LXX and Samaritan Pentateuch would be greatly diminished if sufficiently ancient manuscripts could be found, for it was believed that an original text had once existed for most biblical books. The purity and simplicity of the original was corrupted over the centuries as errors and deliberate changes crept in, eventually leading to the multiplicity evident in the MT, LXX and Samaritan Pentateuch. Faced with this situation, the natural task of the scholar before 1947 was to recover the original text as far as possible. The biblical DSS, however, have made assumptions like these difficult to maintain. With direct access to manuscripts of such antiquity, it now appears that the reality was quite the opposite because the diversity reflected in the DSS is greater than ever. It looks as though the Synagogue and the Church each chose a single edition of the books of the Bible after 70 CE in order to simplify matters. The Samaritan community presumably did the same, although we do not know when.

In light of the above discussion, it is worth considering the implications of the nature of the biblical DSS in one final respect. The oldest biblical manuscript from Qumran dates to around 250 BCE and, as cautioned earlier, we should be wary in extrapolating from such material anything about the state of the biblical text in the preceding period. It is difficult to imagine, however, that the diversity evident in the Qumran documents stemmed from a more homogeneous tradition in the immediately preceding era – between *circa* 550 and 300 BCE. In fact, since most Old Testament writings took shape during this period, it seems likely that from the start they existed in diverse editions. The presence of multiple editions of individual books at Qumran, moreover, makes it difficult to maintain earlier hypotheses that geographical or sectarian factors were what shaped such differences.[22]

If this general picture is accurate, it may be best to give up the whole idea of the original text of the Hebrew Scriptures in favour of the existence of more fluid traditions, some of them oral but others written down. In that case, 1QIsa^a and 1QIsa^b would count as individual written manifestations of a broad and shifting Isaiah tradition. The same would apply to the editions of Jeremiah as evidenced in 4QJer^{a-e}, for they reflect a tradition which was in a state of flux well into the Second Temple period. In short, and inasmuch as the biblical DSS reveal a textual variety unimaginable before 1947, scholars are ceasing to speak of the original text of a given Old Testament book. In many cases, such an original may never have existed.

APOCRYPHA AND PSEUDEPIGRAPHA AT QUMRAN

The biblical books we have just surveyed make up the Hebrew Scriptures or Hebrew Bible of the synagogue. More commonly, of course, they are referred to as the Old Testament – although originally this was an exclusively Christian designation which assumed the existence of a New Testament. The limits of what were to be included in the Jewish Bible were fixed around 100 CE. The decisions taken have remained in force ever since, and the Jewish Publication Society's *Tanakh: the Holy Scriptures* illustrates what has become the standard three-fold arrangement of the Hebrew Bible into the Torah (Law), Nevi'im (Prophets), and Ketuvim (Writings):[23]

Torah	Nevi'im	Ketuvim
Genesis	Joshua	Psalms
Exodus	Judges	Proverbs
Leviticus	1, 2 Samuel	Job
Numbers	1, 2 Kings	Song of Songs
Deuteronomy	Isaiah	Ruth
	Jeremiah	Lamentations
	Ezekiel	Ecclesiastes
	Twelve Minor Prophets	Esther
	(Hosea, Joel, Amos,	Daniel
	Obadiah, Jonah, Micah,	Ezra
	Nahum, Habakkuk,	Nehemiah
	Zephaniah, Haggai,	1, 2 Chronicles
	Zechariah, Malachi)	

Before 70 CE, however, there was no fixed list of authoritative books. As we shall discover in the next section, it is better to picture instead an amorphous pool of scriptural works with the Torah at its centre. The early Christians naturally inherited this state of affairs in the mid-first century CE, and it was only after the destruction of the Temple that they too felt it necessary to define more carefully those books which were biblical. But Jews and Christians had parted company by then, and the various Christian Churches included in their Old Testament a number of works which the Jews had earlier opted to discard.

Some of the books concerned were originally composed in Greek, although many had circulated first in either Hebrew or Aramaic. But it was in their Greek form that they were appropriated by the Church, as with the remainder of the Old Testament. Thus only in manuscripts of the LXX have most of these extra works survived intact to the present day. Allowing for some fluctuation between Churches, a total of sixteen compositions have featured in the Old Testament canon of one Christian Church or another:

Tobit	1 Maccabees
Judith	2 Maccabees
various additions to Esther	1 Esdras
Wisdom of Solomon	Prayer of Manasseh
Ecclesiasticus	Psalm 151
Baruch	3 Maccabees
Epistle or Letter of Jeremiah	2 Esdras
various additions to Daniel	4 Maccabees

Nowadays, these works are usually referred to as the Apocrypha, a term first coined by St Jerome in a pejorative sense.[24] Working in around 400 CE, he was of the opinion that Christians ought to have admitted into their Old Testament only those books contained in the Hebrew Scriptures of the Jews. He therefore sought to persuade his co-religionists that they should discard the additional writings listed above, just as the Jews had done several centuries earlier. As it turned out, the Church authorities of the day did not accept Jerome's conclusion. At the time of the Reformation, however, Protestants took his advice on board, believing that the shorter Hebrew Bible of the synagogue would have been the Bible circulating in Jesus' day. Although they were probably mistaken in this belief, it has been common practice since the Reformation for Protestant and Anglican Bibles to omit the books of the Apocrypha or relegate them to a separate appendix. Roman Catholic and Orthodox Bibles, on the other hand, continue to incorporate them within the main body of the Old Testament, referring to them not as the Apocrypha but as works which are deemed 'Deutero-canonical'.[25]

These historical developments explain the third major difference between English Bibles mentioned in passing at the start of this chapter, for there are essentially three biblical canons: the Jewish, the Roman Catholic or Orthodox, and the Protestant.[26] Again, such variety might surprise those who have always assumed the Bible to be a fixed entity, but, as has hopefully been made clear, the reasons behind it are relatively straightforward.

Returning to the DSS, scholars were excited when the remains of four works from the Apocrypha were found among the manuscripts at Qumran. They were copies of Tobit in Hebrew and Aramaic (4QTob^{a-e}), two portions of Ecclesiasticus in Hebrew (2QSir and part of 11QPs^a), a Hebrew version of Psalm 151 (also in 11QPs^a), as well as a Greek fragment of the Letter of Jeremiah (7QpapLXXEpJer). Before 1947, the first three had only survived in the Greek translation of the LXX. Their presence at Qumran showed that they had circulated during the Second Temple period in an original Semitic language. In relation to Tobit, however, the propensity of the DSS to baffle, as well as to inform, shines out once again. Whereas scholars had long speculated over whether the LXX translation of Tobit was made from a Hebrew or Aramaic original, the DSS yielded both Hebrew and Aramaic editions of the document lying side by side in Cave 4. Rather like 1QIsa^a and 1QIsa^b or 4QJer^{a-e}, it is likely that these alternative Hebrew and Aramaic versions are particular manifestations of a broad and fluid Tobit tradition current in Second Temple times.

There is a final corpus of literature that needs to be considered in this chapter. Scholars usually call it the Pseudepigrapha and it includes a large body of religious works from the last few centuries BCE and first few centuries CE. The writings concerned are all Jewish in origin, though some have had Christian additions incorporated subsequently. With two significant exceptions, none entered into either the Jewish or the Christian Bible. Nevertheless, many were preserved through the ages in obscure languages on the periphery of the Christian Church – thereby explaining how Christian interpolations arose in a number of them.

The name Pseudepigrapha itself is simply a handy term employed by modern scholars and means literally 'false writings'. It expresses a prominent feature of many of the compositions concerned: they are pseudonymous. In other words, although ascribed to one of the heroes of ancient Israel like Abraham, Moses or Ezra, they were actually penned anonymously by Jews living during the last few centuries BCE or the first few centuries CE.[27] In view of their number, it is not possible to list all of the Pseudepigrapha, but included among the principal texts are 1 Enoch, Jubilees, Testaments of the Twelve Patriarchs, Assumption of Moses, Psalms of Solomon, Ascension of Isaiah, and 2 Baruch.[28] Of these, 1 Enoch and Jubilees form part of the Old Testament of the Ethiopic Church.

Apart from several damaged copies of texts relating to the Testaments of the Twelve Patriarchs, the main contribution of the Qumran caves to our understanding of the Pseudepigrapha concerns 1 Enoch and Jubilees. Before 1947, they had survived only in translations of translations passed on by the Church. More precisely, the complete text of both documents had been preserved in an Ethiopic rendering of a Greek translation of the lost Hebrew or Aramaic original. Thanks to the DSS, we now have access to parts of each work in its original language – 1 Enoch in Aramaic (4QEn^{a-f}) and Jubilees in Hebrew (1QJub^{a-b}, 2QJub, 4QJub^{a-h}, 11QJub).[29] Judging by the number of copies at Qumran, both compositions were popular among the community living there. And, because they contain little that can be construed as sectarian, they were doubtless just as popular among many in the wider Jewish community of the Second Temple period.

The second category of DSS, as defined in Chapter 1, can be thought of as comparable to these Pseudepigrapha. Despite being unknown before 1947, they too were probably circulating widely in Second Temple times. In fact, their only distinguishing characteristic seems to be that, unlike books from the Bible, Apocrypha and Pseudepigrapha, they were lost after 70 CE. Like 1QapGen, mentioned earlier in this regard, scholars simply did not know of their existence until recently. Alongside 1QapGen, scraps of works similar to the Pseudepigrapha abound among the DSS – featuring ancient heroes such as Noah, Jacob, Joseph, Joshua, Moses, David, Jeremiah, Ezekiel, and Daniel. The extent of such material has only now begun to be appreciated with the release of fresh Cave 4 texts in 1991. Speculation about prominent biblical heroes, as well as more obscure characters like Qahat and Amram, was evidently popular both with the members of the community at Qumran and many of their contemporaries among the rest of Second Temple Jewry.[30]

THE BOUNDARIES OF THE QUMRAN CANON

The subject of this chapter so far has been rather complicated. If the information on the Bible available before 1947 seemed complex enough, then the situation after the discovery of the DSS might be described as chaotic. Yet, this impression reflects the very nature of the evidence itself. Judging by the plethora of different witnesses among the DSS, the biblical text in the last few centuries of the Second Temple period was in a state of flux, for multiple editions of many biblical works were in circulation. Sometimes the divergences between competing editions were minor, as in 1QIsaᵃ and 1QIsaᵇ, but in other cases they were considerable, as 4QJerᵃ⁻ᵉ demonstrate. In response to this overwhelming diversity, Jews and Christians after 70 CE took it upon themselves to simplify matters: the synagogue defined the MT as its Bible, while the Christian community opted for the LXX tradition. The Samaritans presumably made a similar decision, although we have no direct evidence to suggest when this might have taken place.

As we saw in the last section, moves were also made to limit exactly what books should be included in the Bible, although once again Jewish and Christian leaders decided differently. That is why, taking developments during the Reformation into account, there are three major canons of scripture to this day. It is also why, notwithstanding this variation, we are all used to viewing the Bible as a relatively fixed entity. In contrast, a more open-ended corpus of books was in use in Second Temple times, although the Torah was doubtless at its centre.

It may surprise readers, therefore, to learn that this conclusion is not shared by all scholars. In fact, since the start of serious academic study of the Bible, a different viewpoint has become the norm. This assumes that the traditional Jewish tripartite division of the Hebrew Bible – into the Law, Prophets and Writings – originated in the Second Temple period. According to this reconstruction, not only does the Pentateuch as a fixed authority stem from the sixth or fifth century BCE, but the Prophets was in existence as a defined collection by the second century BCE. A third body of writings, headed by the Psalms, was all but complete by the first century CE, its precise contents being finally settled soon after 70 CE. The evidence adduced to support this thesis seems compelling at first. For example, the prologue to Ecclesiasticus, written in the 130s BCE, speaks of 'the Law itself, the Prophecies, and the rest of the books . . .', while the reference in Luke 24:44

to the 'Law of Moses, the prophets and the psalms' might be taken in the same way.

Nevertheless, a more radical view is now gaining ground among scholars.[31] It holds that the three-fold division of the Jewish Bible was an innovation which occurred after the destruction of the Temple. As already hinted, there were in reality no fixed boundaries outside the Pentateuch beforehand. In Second Temple times, the scriptures consisted primarily of the Torah, God's principal revelation to the people of Israel and their descendants, the Jews, supplemented by an open-ended pool of other works which could be referred to loosely as the 'Prophets'. In support of this alternative reconstruction, it can be pointed out that 'the law and the prophets' is in fact a more usual way of referring to the scriptures in Second Temple literature, especially in the New Testament.[32] In this usage, a prophet was any pious hero from the biblical period up to the return from exile whose words might be construed as coming from God. Accordingly, a prophetic book was any work believed to have been written by one of a long line of holy people – ranging from Enoch and Abraham through Moses, David and Solomon to Isaiah, Jeremiah and Ezra. Even a collection like the Psalms, which functioned as a kind of hymn book for the Temple before 70 CE, could be reckoned as prophetic from this perspective. Associated with King David, one of Israel's greatest heroes, its contents were thought to speak afresh to each new generation, even if not set in the narrowly prophetic genre of Isaiah or Habakkuk. This explains why the writer of Acts 2:30 portrays the Apostle Peter citing Psalm 16 and describing David, its presumed author, as a prophet. It also doubtless explains why the Psalms were so popular at Qumran.[33]

Unfortunately, nowhere do the DSS themselves directly address the issue of a canon, for no catalogue has come to light listing the works which were viewed as authoritative at

Qumran. But two details indirectly support the view outlined above. First, given the multiple copies of 1 Enoch and Jubilees retrieved from Cave 4, it is difficult to avoid concluding that these works were treated as scripture by the community. Both compositions claim to stem from two of Israel's holiest men of old – Enoch and Moses. Assuming this assertion was accepted by the Qumran group, there would have been no reason to view such documents as any less worthy than Isaiah, Psalms or even the Pentateuch itself. Second, some of the sectarian DSS appear to cite words from books which would later be rejected by Jews and by most Christians after 70 CE. The clearest examples are found in the sectarian work known as the Damascus Document. In the Damascus Document 16:3–4, for instance, we find the following reference to the book of Jubilees:

> As for the exact determination of their times to which Israel turns a blind eye, behold it is strictly defined in the *Book of the Divisions of the Times into their Jubilees and Weeks*

These words imply that Jubilees was an authoritative text, presumably because its association with Moses was accepted by the writer of the Damascus Document.[34] A similar case occurs in one of the smaller books of the New Testament, inasmuch as Jude 14–15 appears to refer to a passage from 1 Enoch as though it had scriptural status.

In sum, then, we have learned in this chapter that the DSS reveal a situation prevailing in Second Temple times which was doubly different to what most modern readers of the Bible would suppose. On the one hand, there was no list of books which constituted a definitive Bible with fixed boundaries. Only the Torah seems to have been thought of in these terms, for it contained the very blueprint of Judaism itself. Alongside it circulated an open-ended collection which incorporated all the books later to be defined as part of the Bible by Jews and Christians. But it also encompassed a lot more besides, including books from the Apocrypha and Pseudepigrapha.

The second surprise provided by the DSS concerns the actual words on the page, as it were, of particular compositions. To repeat an earlier observation, divergent editions of various biblical texts existed in the last two centuries BCE and the first century CE. Remarkably, some of them were found lying side by side in the caves at Qumran.

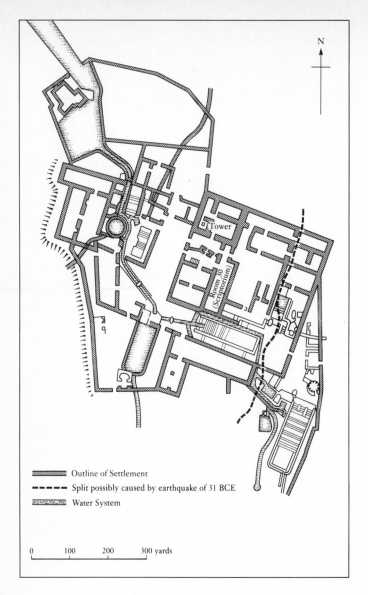

N

Tower

Room 30
(Scriptorium)

Outline of Settlement

Split possibly caused by earthquake of 31 BCE

Water System

0   100   200   300 yards

Plan of Khirbet Qumran

CHAPTER 3

Who Wrote
the Dead Sea Scrolls?

DATING THE DEAD SEA SCROLLS

At the start of this book, the DSS were defined as important Jewish texts from the last three centuries of the Second Temple period. This assertion rests on the findings of carbon dating, palaeography, and archaeology, as well as on references to several historical characters in the sectarian DSS. Before proceeding to examine the contents of the latter in the main body of this chapter, therefore, it is worth spelling out precisely what these other means of inquiry have revealed.

Let us start with carbon dating. Back in 1950, tests on some linen cloth from Cave 1 gave a date of 33 CE – within a 200-year margin of error.[1] Based on the predictable deterioration of carbon's radioactivity, this measurement indirectly confirmed the antiquity of the DSS, especially since a fragment of decomposing manuscript was attached to one of the linen pieces. More recent analysis has taken place through Accelerator Mass Spectrometry, or AMS for short. This improved technique measures the level of carbon more precisely. Tests carried out in 1990–91 on a selection of Qumran texts gave these results:

Text	AMS Result	Palaeographical Date
4QTQahat	388–353 BCE	100–75 BCE
4QPentPara[b]	339–324/209–117 BCE	125–100 BCE
1QIsa[a]	335–327/202–107 BCE	125–100 BCE
4QTLevi	191–155/146–120 BCE	*circa* 100 BCE
4QSam[c]	192–63 BCE	100–75 BCE
11QT[a]	97 BCE–1 CE	*circa* 1 BCE/CE
1QapGen	73 BCE–14 CE	*circa* 1 BCE/CE
1QH	21 BCE–61 CE	50 BCE–70 CE

Even the refined analysis of AMS provides no more than an approximate time span within which a given document was likely to have been copied.[2] As the table indicates, where two samples from a text were analysed under slightly different conditions, some divergences occurred. Nevertheless, the figures show that there can be no serious doubt that the DSS stem from the second half of the Second Temple period. Indeed, further AMS tests conducted on another selection of DSS in 1995 confirmed this broad picture.[3] In particular, it has been shown beyond all reasonable doubt that one of the most important sectarian DSS, 1QpHab, stemmed from the first century BCE.

Long before these AMS tests were carried out, scholars working in the field of palaeography – analysis of the handwriting adopted by ancient scribes – had come to the same conclusion. Although there was little material of a similar age with which to compare the DSS, scholars in the late 1940s and early 1950s surmised that the Qumran documents were probably written between *circa* 200 BCE and 70 CE. As evidence, various similarities and differences were observed in relation to some Aramaic papyri from Egypt, as well as funerary inscriptions from Palestine and the Nash papyrus.[4] Then, in the 1950s and 1960s, documents were unearthed at Wadi ed-Daliyeh, Masada, Murabba'at and Nahal Hever.[5] The fact that some of these manuscripts were dated letters from individuals indirectly confirmed the palaeographers' conclusions. Albeit historically unconnected, the handwriting of the material from Qumran could be neatly slotted between the fourth-century writing of the Wadi ed-Daliyeh texts, on the one hand, and the Murabba'at and Nahal Hever texts, on the other. Moreover, in support of the general picture that had emerged from palaeography, AMS tests carried out on some of these non-Qumran samples in 1990–91 yielded the following results:

Text	AMS Result	Internal Date
Wadi ed-Daliyeh	405–354/306–231 BCE	352 BCE
Wadi Murabba'at	69–136 CE	134 CE

The correlation evident between the AMS results and the internal dates confirms the outer limits of the palaeographers' framework and, by implication, the placing of the Qumran manuscripts in between them.

As a result of studies of this kind, every Qumran manuscript can be roughly classified in one of three ways on the basis of its handwriting: archaic (*circa* 250–150 BCE), Hasmonean (*circa* 150–30 BCE), and Herodian (*circa* 30 BCE–70 CE).[6] Most DSS are either late Hasmonean or Herodian.

The perimeters set by carbon dating and palaeography were further confirmed by archaeology, for five seasons of excavation at Qumran yielded clear general results.[7] The site had been settled during Israelite times but was destroyed towards the end of the seventh century BCE. It was then reoccupied in the Second Temple period. Examination of what archaeologists call the material culture – building and cemetery remains, pottery, coins – allowed this second phase of habitation to be further subdivided. In what was labelled Period Ia, the initial resettlement took place in the second half of the second century BCE, when buildings were restored and new rooms added. During Period Ib which followed, the site was expanded to include a tower, dining facilities, an assembly room and a complex water system. These features suggest that the site could have provided communal facilities for up to two hundred people at any one time, although surrounding caves served as living quarters and limited excavations of the cemetery next to Qumran show it is likely that most of these inhabitants were male. On the basis of coins found in the relevant layer of the ruins, Period Ib stretched from *circa* 100 BCE until the reign of Herod the Great (37–4 BCE). There is some debate as to whether Qumran was then abandoned for several decades. According to Josephus, an earthquake struck Judaea in 31 BCE and its impact could explain traces of structural damage.[8] In any case, coin finds suggest that Period II began at the start of the first century CE. Associated with it are the famous table and the inkwells which de Vaux reckoned to be part of a 'scriptorium' – a room where manuscripts were copied or composed.[9]

Finally, Period III commenced with the arrival of Roman forces in the vicinity. We know from elsewhere that the Tenth Legion captured Jericho around 68 CE and, in light of Roman coins left behind, Qumran was doubtless overrun too as part of the military campaign to quash the First Revolt. As for the Romans, they remained at the settlement for several years because a few pockets of resistance held out in the desert.

Overall, the degree of correlation between the three separate means of inquiry just described is remarkable. It shows that Qumran was occupied from the second half of the second century BCE until 68 CE. That a few biblical manuscripts among the DSS are older is easily explained by the likelihood that those who first settled at Qumran brought with them documents already in their possession.

The cumulative force of all this evidence is bolstered by a further feature, for a handful of DSS actually name historical personages. Thus, 4QpNah refers to two Greek kings of Syria who are almost certainly Antiochus IV (174–164 BCE) and Demetrius III (92–89 BCE). Again, the damaged 4QCalendar C refers to Salome, the Jewish queen who ruled Judaea between 76 and 67 BCE, and to a certain Aemilius, better known as Aemilius Scaurus, the first Roman governor of Syria between 65 and 62 BCE. Combined with the results of carbon dating, palaeography and archaeology, these references leave us in no doubt that the context for understanding the DSS is that of the last two or three hundred years of the Second Temple period. Accordingly, let us turn to these three centuries in more detail.

UNDERSTANDING THE SECOND TEMPLE PERIOD

The Second Temple period covers roughly six centuries of Jewish history from the return of the Babylonian exiles in the sixth century BCE to the destruction of the Temple in 70 CE. A variety of literary sources allows us to reconstruct the history of the period in broad outline: late biblical books, the Apocrypha and Pseudepigrapha, the DSS, the New Testament, and the works of Philo and Josephus. Most of this material relates only to the last three hundred years of Second Temple times and, because the DSS slot neatly between *circa* 250 BCE and

70 CE, it makes sense for us to concentrate on the second half of the Second Temple period in the following discussion. Of all the relevant literature, Daniel, 1 Maccabees and the writings of Josephus are most useful in gaining a historical overview, while other compositions provide sporadic supplementary insights.[10]

As remarked in Chapter 1, the conquest of Judaea by Alexander the Great had long-lasting repercussions for the Jews and Judaism. After his death in 323 BCE, two opposing empires emerged out of his vast kingdom: the Ptolemaic Empire in Egypt, and the Seleucid Empire, including what is now Lebanon and Syria.[11] The small province of Judaea continued under Egyptian control for most of the third century BCE, but the Seleucids wrested it from the Ptolemies in around 200 BCE. The sensibilities of both governments, as well as of Alexander before them, can be described as Greek or 'Hellenistic'. Put another way, they were very much influenced by Hellenism – Greek language, customs and ideas. By the second century, accordingly, a number of Greek cities or *poleis* (singular, *polis*) had been established on the Mediterranean coast (Gaza, Ascalon, Joppa, Dor and Ptolemais) and inland (Philadelphia, Scythopolis and Samaria – later renamed Sebaste). The inhabitants of these largely independent city-states, headed by a *boule* or legislative council, were left to organize themselves according to a semi-democratic structure; they were also encouraged to adopt Greek language and social customs – and to make room for Greek deities in their religious system.

Such developments inevitably had a slow Hellenizing impact on the indigenous people living nearby, including Judaea. As a result, divisions over how to respond to growing Hellenization emerged among Jews from the start of the second century BCE. In Ecclesiasticus 41:8, for instance, the early second-century author complains about his fellow Jews who had 'forsaken the law of the Most High God'. A similar concern in the book of

Jubilees, written soon afterwards, is evident in its vehement exhortation to keep the Sabbath and observe the rite of circumcision.

Tensions came to a head during the reign of the Seleucid monarch Antiochus IV Epiphanes (175–164 BCE). Being short of funds in the imperial treasury, he accepted a bribe in 175 BCE from a certain Jesus, whose brother was the High Priest in Jerusalem. In return, this Jesus, who preferred the Greek name Jason, was given the High Priesthood in place of his brother. Jason then set about turning Jerusalem into a *polis*, establishing institutions for inculcating Jewish youth with Greek intellectual and sporting ideals. Many were offended by these developments, as 1 Maccabees 1:11–15 makes clear:

> [11]In those days certain renegades came out from Israel and misled many, saying, 'Let us go and make a covenant with the Gentiles around us, for since we separated from them many disasters have come upon us.' [12]This proposal pleased them, [13]and some of the people eagerly went to the king, who authorized them to observe the ordinances of the Gentiles. [14]So they built a gymnasium in Jerusalem, according to Gentile custom, [15]and removed the marks of circumcision, and abandoned the holy covenant. They joined with the Gentiles and sold themselves to do evil.

This passage shows there was a strong Hellenizing faction within Jerusalem in the mid-second century BCE. In the eyes of traditionalists, however, its desire to absorb Greek customs and values was nothing short of a dilution of Judaism. Nevertheless, the High Priest's position was purchased again in 172 BCE by another Greek enthusiast called Menelaus. The changes introduced included nude participation in athletics – thereby flouting the biblical taboo against nakedness and causing some Jewish embarrassment over circumcision, which was viewed by Greeks as a rather crude practice.

Then, events took a turn for the worse. Not only did Antiochus IV raid the Temple funds in Jerusalem, but in 167 BCE he set about eradicating the practice of Judaism altogether. Such religious persecution was unheard of in the ancient world and scholars disagree as to its causes. Antiochus was probably quashing rival supporters of Jason and Menelaus, rather than opposing Judaism itself; he may also have been angered by a recent military withdrawal from Egypt forced on him by the Romans. In any case, Antiochus IV banned Jewish customs on pain of death. Worse still, pagan sacrifice was introduced into the Temple, which was rededicated to the Greek god Olympian Zeus. This particular sacrilege lies behind the reference to the 'abomination that makes desolate' in Daniel 11:31. Under these circumstances, many Jews simply acquiesced (1 Maccabees 2:23), while others hoped for divine intervention (Daniel 7–12). Yet others embarked on a course of violent resistance to Antiochus IV's measures. They were led by a pious priest from Modein called Mattathias and his five sons – most notably Judah (or Judas), Jonathan, and Simon. Judah gained the nickname 'Maccabee', of uncertain meaning, and so the brothers are often referred to collectively as the Maccabees.

These Maccabees, aided by the obscure Hasideans or 'pious ones' mentioned in 1 Maccabees 2:42, slowly undermined the Seleucid army by employing the tactics of guerrilla warfare. As the Seleucids sent reinforcements to quell the revolt, their armies were outwitted, ambushed and defeated by the Maccabees' supporters, who were then able to confiscate their opponents' weaponry. In 164 BCE, Judah Maccabee succeeded in his main aim of restoring proper Jewish worship to the Jerusalem Temple.[12] Then, with the accession of Antiochus V to the Seleucid throne, the oppressive measures of his predecessor were rescinded. As life returned to normal, not surprisingly, the impetus behind the Maccabean campaign faded. A peace deal was struck between Antiochus V and the Jews, marginalizing the Maccabees, who withdrew to the small town of Michmash.

Some years later, two rival claimants to the Seleucid throne each tried to gain the military support of the Maccabees. Jonathan Maccabee eventually threw his lot in with Demetrius I in return for the High Priesthood. His appointment in 152 BCE must have earned him many enemies, for neither Jonathan nor his brothers were from the priestly family descended from Zadok which held the exclusive right to supply High Priests. Since no one was in a powerful enough position to challenge him, however, Jonathan's rule continued until he was captured through trickery by a foreign general and executed in 143 BCE. Thereupon, his brother, Simon, took over and, with the weakening of the Seleucid empire, declared the small province of Judaea an independent state in 141 BCE. Against this background, 1 Maccabees 14:4,12 glorifies his achievements:

> [4]The land had rest all the days of Simon.
>
> He sought the good of his nation;
>
> his rule was pleasing to them,
>
> as was the honour shown him, all his days . . .
>
> [12]All the people sat under their own vines and fig trees,
>
> and there was none to make them afraid.

Writing propaganda for the Maccabees' successors in around 100 BCE, the author deliberately echoes the glorious days of King Solomon in his final sentence.[13]

Simon was succeeded by his son and subsequent offspring. Like Jonathan and Simon Maccabee, they combined the role of High Priest with that of secular ruler; they are collectively known as the Hasmoneans.[14] The first three Hasmoneans were skilful in military matters: John Hyrcanus I (134–104 BCE),

Aristobulus I (104–103 BCE) and Alexander Jannaeus (103–76 BCE). Between them, they added to the Jewish state Samaria, Idumea, Peraea, Galilee, the *poleis* on the Mediterranean coast, as well as territory to the north-east of the Sea of Galilee.[15] As part of the process, some of the non-Jewish population was expelled or converted. So thorough was this policy that the Idumeans, converted under Hyrcanus I, and the non-Jewish inhabitants of Galilee, forcibly circumcised by Aristobulus I, remained Jewish after the Hasmonean state fell to Rome in 63 BCE.[16]

Such religious zeal helped consolidate the Hasmonean kingdom. But, whereas Antiochus IV had sought to eradicate Judaism, the Hasmoneans also managed to forge a workable Jewish–Greek synthesis. Many practical aspects of public and private life under the Hasmonean dynasty were therefore influenced by Hellenism. Their coins, for example, show the traditional Hebrew name of the High Priest on one side, while the reverse bears his Greek secular title. Again, the remains of the recently excavated Hasmonean palace at Jericho combine the best of Hellenistic artistry with the provision of ritual baths so that the High Priest could maintain his purity in line with the law of Moses. Among the wider populace, burial customs exhibit a similar fusion of cultures.

However, it should not be supposed that everyone was content. Nor is it coincidental that Josephus first mentions three distinct religious parties – the Sadducees, Pharisees and Essenes – in his accounts of the Maccabees and Hasmoneans. Indeed, while the Sadducees largely supported the Hasmonean dynasty, Jonathan Maccabee's scandalous assumption of the High Priesthood in 152 BCE was probably an important factor in the formation of the Essenes. The position of the Pharisees on specific issues is less easy to determine. But Josephus informs us that ordinary people supported their interpretation of the Law in preference to that of the Sadducees.

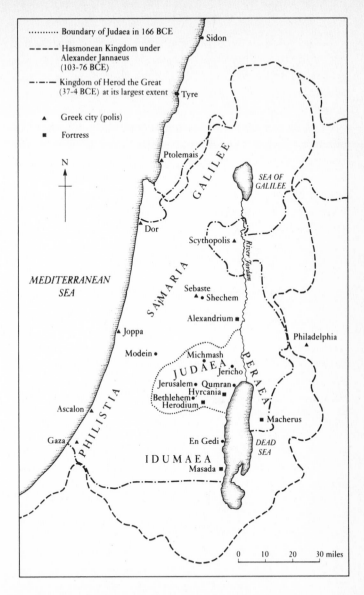

The Hasmonean and Herodian Kingdoms

Josephus also tells us that the wider populace was capable of making its feelings known in a more dramatic fashion from time to time. When Alexander Jannaeus was officiating as High Priest one year at the Feast of Tabernacles, for example, the crowds of pilgrims in the Temple gave vent to their disaffection by pelting him with ceremonial fruit.[17] As his standing plummeted even further among the common people, the Pharisees were implicated in a plot to call on the Seleucid King Demetrius III to help unseat him around 88 BCE. The attempted coup failed, and Jannaeus had eight hundred of his Pharisaic opponents crucified.[18] This cruel act is alluded to in 4QpNah 1:6–7:[19]

> *[And chokes prey for its lionesses; and it fills] its caves [with prey] and its dens with victims* (ii, 12a–b).
>
> Interpreted, this concerns the furious young lion [who executes revenge] on those who seek smooth things and hangs men alive . . .

In this passage, which is preceded by mention of '[Deme]trius king of Greece', the 'furious young lion' is certainly Jannaeus. Because we know from Josephus that his victims were Pharisees, 'those who seek smooth things' must describe the sect's Pharisaic opponents, who were thought to engage in lax or 'smooth' interpretations of the Law. In what follows, 4QpNah 2:2 also dubs the Pharisees as Ephraim, while the corresponding term, 'Manasseh', seems to be a nickname for the Sadducees.

After Jannaeus' death, his wife, Salome Alexandra, became queen; the High Priesthood, open only to males, went to their son Hyrcanus II. On the advice of her late husband, Salome allied herself with the Pharisees and we are told that her reign was peaceful. But things began to deteriorate with her death in 67 BCE. Aristobulus II, younger brother of Hyrcanus II, seized the High Priesthood and set himself up as king. Naturally, this was not to the liking of Hyrcanus II and the two rivals became locked in confrontation.

To break the stalemate, both sides petitioned Rome for help. Their competing requests enabled the Roman general Pompey to take Jerusalem in 63 BCE, thereby rendering the Jewish state a puppet kingdom answerable to Rome. After the removal of the Greek cities on the Mediterranean coast from Jewish jurisdiction and the restoration of their semi-autonomous status, Aristobulus II was deposed and Hyrcanus II left in charge. Some time later, one of Hyrcanus' advisers, an Idumean convert called Antipater, was made overseer of Judaea. Thanks to his influence within the court of the weak client king, his sons Phasael and Herod also achieved prominent positions in the administration of Jerusalem and Galilee. Even after Antipater's assassination in 42 BCE, and despite opposition among Jerusalem's aristocracy, Phasael and Herod seemed destined for success, especially in view of their father's good relations with Rome. But then, with the invasion of Judaea from the east by the Parthians in 40 BCE, the situation changed dramatically. The Parthians, Rome's main rival in the region, set up Antigonus, son of Aristobulus II, as High Priest and King in Jerusalem.

Herod fled to Rome, where he was declared King of Judaea by the Senate. Returning with an army, he recaptured Jerusalem in 37 BCE and brought Hasmonean rule to an end. With Roman backing, he subsequently reigned for some thirty years over a territory similar in size to the Hasmonean kingdom at its greatest. Usually, of course, he is referred to as Herod the Great.[20] His reign was a mixture of opposites, coupling prosperity and a massive building programme with domestic strife and political intrigue. To offset his image as the son of a converted Idumean and therefore a kind of impostor, Herod tried to present himself as a pious adherent of Jewish practice and belief. Most notably, he embarked on a massive expansion of the Jerusalem Temple to court the favour of the Jews. But he also lavished substantial sums on pagan temples and other Hellenistic institutions in non-Jewish towns to win the loyalty of their inhabitants. He spent a vast amount of money constructing the city port of Caesarea, for example, as a tribute to Emperor Augustus Caesar. To guard against insurrection, he also ensured he had impressive fortresses – especially Masada, Herodium, Alexandrium, Hyrcania and Macherus. Indeed, as Herod became increasingly paranoid about plots against him towards the end of his reign, he ordered the execution or assassination of many members of his family, including his wife and sons.

After his own death in 4 BCE, Herod's kingdom was divided among his three remaining sons.[21] Herod Antipas took control of Galilee and Peraea, while Philip ruled the territory to the north-east of the Sea of Galilee. Judaea and Samaria were given to Herod Archelaus. Due to his incompetence, however, Archelaus was sacked by the Romans in 6 CE. His inheritance was turned into a Roman province under the rule of a series of prefects – the most famous being Pontius Pilate who was responsible for executing Jesus.[22] Between 41 and 44 CE, Herod the Great's grandson, Agrippa I, was appointed king over all of what had been his grandfather's territory. But after his untimely death, the whole region came under direct Roman rule again – this time under officials called procurators.

In large measure, the despicable behaviour of the procurators led to the First Revolt of the Jews against Rome. It began in 66 CE when Procurator Gessius Florus (64–66 CE) took money from the Temple for alleged unpaid taxes. This sort of incident had happened before, but sensitivities were particularly high after a recent dispute between the Jewish and Greek inhabitants of Caesarea in which the procurator had sided with the majority non-Jewish population. When, therefore, following his raid on the Temple, some among the crowds in Jerusalem mockingly made a collection for poor Florus, only to be butchered in the streets by his soldiers, Jewish frustration and anger boiled over, plunging the whole country into rebellion. Not surprisingly, Roman might quashed the Revolt, helped by internal divisions on the Jewish side. Jerusalem and its Temple were destroyed in the process, bringing the Second Temple period to a close in 70 CE. Nearly one thousand rebels held out in the desert fortress of Masada, but in 74 CE they committed mass suicide rather than admit defeat.[23]

Although there was a Second Revolt against Rome between 132 and 135 CE, likewise crushed by superior forces, the defeat of the rebels in 70 CE precipitated one of the most important turning points in Judaism. With the loss of the Temple and priesthood, Jewish religion turned its attention almost exclusively on the Torah. Thus was born what experts usually call Rabbinic Judaism, finding classic expression in the Mishnah (200 CE) and the Babylonian Talmud (*circa* 550 CE), and undergoing further elaboration in medieval times by famous rabbis like Rashi and Maimonides. We shall have an opportunity to return to the Rabbinic period briefly in Chapter 4.

DID THE ESSENES WRITE THE DEAD SEA SCROLLS?

The history of the Second Temple period, as outlined above, supplies the framework necessary for making sense of the sectarian DSS. Before explaining how, we shall describe the sources on the Essenes available before 1947 and, given the obvious parallels in the sectarian DSS, see why scholars characterize the latter as Essene in origin.

Prior to the discovery of the DSS, scholars drew their picture of the Essenes from the accounts of two first-century Jewish writers, Philo and Josephus, who are counted among the classical authors of the ancient world.[24] Josephus also furnishes us with details of the other Second Temple religious groupings, especially the Pharisees and Sadducees. In one passage, he makes a rare general characterization of the three major parties:[25]

> As for the Pharisees, they say that certain events are the work of Fate, but not all . . . The sect of the Essenes, however, declares that Fate is mistress of all things, and that nothing befalls men unless it be in accordance with her decree. But the Sadducees do away with Fate, holding . . . that all things lie within our own power . . .

Despite being dressed up in the language of Fate, which would have suited his Greek and Roman readers, there is no reason to doubt Josephus' basic point here: the Essenes believed everything to be foreordained by God, while the Sadducees held the opposite view and the Pharisees took up a midway position.

Turning to specific details, both Philo and Josephus concur on a range of defining characteristics of the Essenes. Numbering some four thousand, they were devout Jews who avoided contact with the Temple and treated their own worship of God as a kind of substitute. After a preliminary year, a potential member could participate in the group's purificatory rituals, but full membership was only achieved with two further years of training. Then, the new member vowed to adhere to the sect's interpretation of the Torah and not to divulge any of its secrets to the uninitiated. According to Josephus, his goods were absorbed into the communal fund:[26]

> Riches they despise, and their community of goods is truly admirable . . . They have a law that new members on admission to the sect shall confiscate their property to the order . . . the individual's possessions join the

common stock and all, like brothers, enjoy a single patrimony.

From this point on, the new sectarian could partake in the community's ritual baths and communal meals:[27]

> ... they ... bathe their bodies in cold water. After this purification, they assemble in a private apartment which none of the uninitiated is permitted to enter; pure now themselves, they repair to the refectory, as to some sacred shrine ... Before meat the priest says a grace, and none may partake until after the prayer.

As this passage implies, the Essenes were concerned with ritual purity. They also kept the Sabbath strictly and maintained an interest in healing through plants and stones. The latter feature could be linked to the name Essene, possibly derived from the Aramaic word *asayya*, meaning 'healers'. Both Philo and Josephus further state that the Essenes were celibate males, although Josephus adds that there was a branch of the sect that did marry.[28] Josephus also informs us of an unusual detail by saying that the Essenes were 'careful not to spit into the midst of the company or to the right' (*Jewish War*, 2.147).

A third source on the Essenes available before 1947 was the work of a non-Jew, the Roman geographer Pliny the Elder (23–79 CE). It is worth citing his short notice from the *Natural History*:[29]

> On the west side of the Dead Sea ... is the solitary tribe of the Essenes, which is remarkable beyond all the other tribes in the whole world, as it has no women and has renounced all sexual desire, has no money, and has only palm trees for company. Day by day the throng of refugees is recruited to an equal number by numerous accessions of persons tired of life and driven thither by the waves of fortune to adopt their manners.

> Thus through thousands of ages . . . a race in which
> no one is born lives on for ever: so prolific for their
> advantage is other men's weariness of life!
>
> Lying below the Essenes was formerly the town of
> Engedi, second only to Jerusalem in the fertility of its
> land and in its groves of palm-trees, but now like
> Jerusalem a heap of ashes. Next comes Masada, a fort-
> ress on a rock, itself also not far from the Dead Sea.

Not only does this passage echo the celibacy and communism
described by Philo and Josephus, but it also directs us to the
western shore of the Dead Sea near Engedi. This location must
surely be Khirbet Qumran. Certainly, the sectarian DSS from
the surrounding caves reflect a group remarkably close to the
picture painted of the Essenes by Philo and Josephus. The best
way to illustrate this is to highlight several distinct overlaps.

Parallel to Josephus' description, cited above, a belief in the
predetermined nature of all things comes across from a range
of sectarian DSS. 1QS 3:15–16 provides a good example:

> From the God of knowledge comes all that is and shall
> be. Before ever they existed He established their whole
> design, and when, as ordained for them, they come
> into being, it is in accord with His glorious design
> that they accomplish their task without change.

The same emphasis crops up in the Damascus Document 2:6–
10 and 1QH 1:7–8. Numerous documents also make it clear
that the group concerned had formed out of a pious desire to
lead a devout life. Like the Essenes of Philo and Josephus,
members underwent a period of training. According to the
Damascus Document 6:11–14, they also shunned the Temple
in Jerusalem:

> None of those brought into the Covenant shall enter
> the Temple to light His altar in vain. They shall bar

the door, forasmuch as God said, *Who among you will bar its door?* And, *You shall not light my altar in vain* (Mal. i, 10)

More positively, 1QS 6:18–23 expresses a parallel commitment to communal ownership and a common pure meal:

> And if it be his destiny, according to the judgement of the Priests and the multitude of the men of their Covenant, to enter the company of the Community, his property and earnings shall be handed over to the Bursar of the Congregation who shall register it to his account and shall not spend it for the Congregation ... But when the second year has passed, he shall be examined, and if it be his destiny, according to the judgement of the Congregation, to enter the Community, then he shall be inscribed among his brethren in the order of his rank for the Law, and for justice, and for the pure Meal; his property shall be merged and he shall offer his counsel and judgement to the Community.

This excerpt stresses the centrality of the group's rigid hierarchy, according to which each member was graded every year in line with his spiritual standing. The priests and, according to some documents, the sons of Zadok seem to have held an elevated position within this hierarchical structure.

A final example relates to Josephus' mention of the sect's unusual rule against spitting. The same prohibition is found in 1QS 7:13 and, although the injunction features in Jewish writings after 70 CE too, its appearance in a sectarian DSS seems too specific – not to say odd – to be merely coincidental.

These and other parallels are ample demonstration of both general and detailed links between the sectarian DSS and the

Essenes of Philo and Josephus. However, various contradictions also exist. Some can be found within the DSS themselves, others in the classical accounts, while the two bodies of literature taken together exhibit further discrepancies. Such disagreements might seem to undermine the hypothesis that the DSS constituted an Essene library. In reality, all serious difficulties of this kind can be explained by one of three factors.

The first is development over time. During the community's two-hundred-year existence at Qumran, it must have evolved in some aspects of its organization and outlook. After the group's initial formation, for instance, secondary satellite communities may have come into existence. Such a development is one way of accounting for differences in the detail of the rules in 1QS and the Damascus Document. It could also account for the celibacy apparently assumed in 1QS, while the Damascus Document presupposes that some of the sect's members married.[30] Similarly, organizational changes accompanying the growth of the sect may explain why the priestly sons of Zadok are more prominent in some documents than in others.

A second factor concerns the perspective of the authors. Philo and Josephus only had relatively superficial knowledge of the Essenes. Even if we accept Josephus' claim to have tried the sect out before becoming a Pharisee, he was never a fully-fledged member.[31] While the generality of his descriptions is for the most part reliable, details found in the sectarian DSS are probably more trustworthy when differences emerge. The probationary period described in 1QS, for example, is more likely to be accurate than Josephus' simpler divergent account.

Thirdly, what about the intended audiences? While most of the sectarian DSS were directed at initiates, the writings of Philo, Josephus and Pliny were aimed at a mixed Jewish–Gentile readership, none of whom were Essenes. Understandably, the three authors tailor-made what they wrote for their audience. That much is evident when Josephus presents the Essenes as similar to the Pythagoreans (*Antiquities of the Jews*, 15.371), just as the Pharisees are likened to the Stoics (*Life*, 12). Both comparisons, it hardly needs to be stated, should be taken with more than a pinch of salt.[32] The ethos of the sectarian DSS, in contrast, is more recognizably Jewish. The documents also contain an exhortatory passion which, while lacking in the classical sources, is to be expected of a zealous religious community.

In sum, the evidence reviewed above renders overwhelming the case for identifying the group behind the DSS as some kind of Essene community. It is now time to look at the sectarian documents in more detail.

SURVEY OF THE SECTARIAN DEAD SEA SCROLLS

Space will not allow us to describe even a majority of the manuscripts.[33] Instead, we shall examine the most important documents across four categories: Rules, Bible Interpretation, Hymns and Liturgies, and Miscellaneous compositions. We shall then be in a position in the next section to consider in a more systematic fashion the history, beliefs and practices of the Qumran community.

I *Rules*

What scholars call the Rules comprise six important documents regulating the life of the community behind the DSS. They also express the group's main aims and provide clues as to its origins.

The first is the so-called Community Rule or Manual of Discipline (1QS), removed from Cave 1 back in 1947.

Although, palaeographically speaking, 1QS was probably written in the early first century BCE, the remains of copies from Cave 4 (4QS^{a-j}) suggest portions of the work once existed separately and stemmed from the sect's formative days in the second century BCE. The central core (1QS 5–9) lists regulations for new members and their property. There are also numerous disciplinary rules, as 1QS 7:17–19 illustrates:

> Whoever has gone about slandering his companion shall be excluded from the pure Meal of the Congregation for one year and shall do penance. But whoever has slandered the Congregation shall be expelled from among them and shall return no more.

Preceding the regulatory core stands a liturgical section and a spiritual instruction (1QS 1–4), while after it come guidance and a hymn for the Master, one of the community's leaders (1QS 9–11).

Another important composition from the sect's early days is the Damascus Document. First discovered in 1896 in Cairo amid a large cache of documents retrieved from an ancient synagogue, a longer edition subsequently turned up in three Qumran caves. No one really knows how the work had found its way to Egypt, but scholars had to depend on the Cairo text until the release of fresh DSS in the autumn of 1991. Now, the most important Qumran copies of the Damascus Document in the form of 4QD^{a-h} are freely available. Like the Cairo text, usually referred to as CD (C = Cairo and D = Damascus), they contain both exhortatory material and laws. The former presents the sect as the true Israel, while all outsiders are deemed to be lost to Satan or Belial. Several cryptic names appear (the Teacher of Righteousness, the Scoffer and the Spouter of Lies) and the place-name Damascus also features. The Teacher of Righteousness is doubtless the founder of the community behind the sectarian DSS, while the Scoffer and the Spouter of Lies are widely held to be alternative nicknames for an individual who deserted the sect in its early stages with a following of his own.

As for the laws in CD and 4QD^{a-h}, they are similar to those in 1QS, although there are numerous discrepancies in specific details. Consequently, it is also widely held that, while 1QS regulated celibate male sectarians living around the Qumran headquarters of the movement, CD was intended for secondary satellite communities or 'camps' in towns elsewhere. If correct, this reconstruction means that those Essenes based at the Qumran centre committed themselves to living without wives according to the sect's strictest interpretation of the Law, as set out in 1QS; they shunned all association with outsiders and refused to participate in the services of the Temple in Jerusalem. Essenes living in the secondary 'camps', in contrast, married and had children; they also countenanced minimal contact with Jews outside the movement for the purposes of trade and may even have allowed limited attendance at the Temple.

The next composition to mention is Miqsat Ma'ase ha-Torah (Some Precepts of the Law) or 4QMMT^{a-f}. Although the subject of much speculation beforehand, this text only entered the public domain in 1991 with the release of outstanding Cave 4 material. The work discusses various legal matters relating to ritual purity and the correct calculation of the calendar. Moreover, it seeks to convince an external leader (addressed as 'you') of the legal positions advocated by the author's community ('we'), in opposition to a third party with different views ('they'):[34]

Remember David, that he was a man of piety who was also [26]delivered from many troubles and pardoned. Also, we have written to you about [27]some precepts of the Law which we think will be beneficial for you and for your people. For we have seen [28]that prudence and knowledge of the Law are with you. Consider all these matters and ask him to straighten [29]your counsel and remove from you evil thoughts and the counsel of Belial. [30]Then you will rejoice at the end of time by finding that some of our sayings are correct.

The official editors have characterized 4QMMT as a letter from the Teacher of Righteousness to the Wicked Priest – an opponent who features prominently in 1QpHab – in the formative days of the sect.[35] This conclusion is somewhat premature, but it does seem safe to say that 'we' stands for the sect behind the sectarian DSS, while, given the comparison with King David, 'you' represents the Maccabean or early Hasmonean authorities in Jerusalem.

Two further compositions among the Rules deal with matters relating to the end of the world. The longest is the War Scroll or War Rule (1QM), also extant in the remains of six copies from Cave 4 (4QM^{a-f}). It pictures a forty-year battle as the end of time approaches, during the course of which the community will move to Jerusalem to restore pure worship in the Temple. The whole world will then be conquered by the forces of good, and this will be followed by celebrations and praises. Unfortunately, it is not spelled out exactly what will happen next.[36] But it is clear that, while weapons and soldiers do feature, the forty-year battle is as much spiritual as military. Only God's intervention wins the day and, according to 1QM 7:1–3, it matters little that the middle-aged and elderly do the fighting, while the young carry the baggage:

The men of the army shall be from forty to fifty years old ... The despoilers of the slain, the plunderers of booty, the cleansers of the land, the keepers of the

Fragments of Tobit in Aramaic from Cave 4 (4QTob^bar) (*Israel Antiquities Authority*)

Fragments of Jubilees from Cave 4 (4QJub^d) (*Israel Antiquities Authority*)

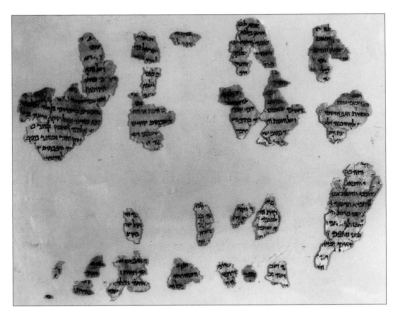

Fragments of a sectarian work called Miqsat Ma'ase ha-Torah (4QMMT^d) (*Israel Antiquities Authority*)

Scroll jars discovered by Bedouin in Cave 1 (*Israel Antiquities Authority*)

Several columns or sections of the sectarian Habbakuk Commentary from Cave 1 (1QpHab) (*Israel Museum/David Harris*)

Section of the longest Dead Sea Scroll called the Temple Scroll from Cave 11 (11QT^a) (*Israel Museum*)

Section of the long Isaiah Scroll from Cave 1 (1QIsa^a) (*Israel Musuem*)

Westerly view towards Cave 4, from the edge of the outcrop on which lies
Khirbet Qumran (© *Jonathan Campbell*)

LEFT A cistern at Khirbet Qumran, probably split by the earthquake of 31 BCE (© *Jonathan Campbell*)

BELOW Southerly view over the ruins of Khirbet Qumran (© *Jonathan Campbell*)

baggage, and those who furnish the provisions shall be from twenty-five to thirty years old.

Because 1QM employs imagery derived from Roman military practice, the work must have been composed after the Roman conquest of Palestine in 63 BCE.

Another text addressing the last days is the Messianic Rule (1QSa). Concerned with Jews who will join the sect during the final war against the nations, it gives instructions for their education. 1QSa 2:11–17 also describes an eschatological banquet attended by two anointed figures:

> When God will have engendered the (Priest-)Messiah, he shall come [at] the head of the whole congregation of Israel with all [his brethren, the sons] of Aaron the Priests, [those called] to the assembly, the men of renown; and they shall sit [before him, each man] in the order of his dignity. And then [the Mess]iah of Israel shall [come], and the chiefs of the [clans of Israel] shall sit before him, [each] in the order of his dignity, according to [his place] in their camps and marches.

These two messianic characters feature in 1QS and CD, too.

Finally, mention should be made of the lengthy Temple Scroll (11QT^a), although its status as a sectarian composition is doubted by some. Concerned with the Temple and its worship, the document harmonizes divergent duplicate laws in the Torah. It is more than a mere compendium of biblical law, however, and a number of links with CD and other texts favour a sectarian origin.[37] Most remarkably, the whole composition is set in the first person and presented as a direct revelation from God to Moses and the people of Israel shortly after their miraculous exodus from Egypt. The following parallel arrangement of Deuteronomy 17:14–16 and 11QT 56:12–18 illustrates well what is involved:[38]

NRSV	11QT
[14]When you have come into the land that the LORD your God is giving you, and have taken possession of it and settled in it, and you say, 'I will set a king over me, like all the nations that are around me,' [15]you may indeed set over you a king whom the LORD your God will choose. One of your own community you may set as king over you; you are not permitted to put a foreigner over you, who is not of your own community. [16]Even so, he must not acquire many horses for himself, or return the people to Egypt in order to acquire more horses, since the LORD has said to you, 'You must never return that way again.'	When you have come into the land that I am giving you, and have taken possession of it and settled in it, and you say, 'I will set a king over me, like all the nations that are around me,' you may indeed set over you a king whom I will choose. One of your own community you may set as king over you; you shall not put a foreigner over you, who is not of your own community. Even so, he must not acquire many horses for himself, or return the people to Egypt *for war* in order to acquire *for himself* more horses, *and silver and gold*, since I have said to you, 'You must never return that way again.'

In the 11QT equivalent, Deuteronomy 17:14–20 is replicated almost exactly. But, as can be seen, God speaks in the first person for dramatic effect, whereas the biblical account simply has Moses report the divine commands in the third person. By way of supplementary interpretation, 11QT has added several words, including 'for war', as indicated in italics. Since some biblical figures, like King Solomon, were known to have traded with Egypt, and because many Second Temple Jews had settled there, these extra words show the writer of 11QT believed it was only a return to Egypt for military action that was forbidden – not for ordinary commercial or residential purposes.

II *Bible Interpretation*

Although the Rules sporadically cite the Bible, the second class of sectarian literature does so more deliberately. The aim is to lend weight to the sect's teachings, as we shall now see.

The best preserved interpretation of a particular biblical book is the Pesher or Commentary on Habakkuk (1QpHab). Its thirteen columns comment verse by verse on Habakkuk 1–2, frequently employing the Hebrew term *pesher*, meaning 'interpretation'. Prominent is the Teacher of Righteousness, the inspired founder and leader of the community behind the document, as 1QpHab 7:3–5, after a citation of Habakkuk 2:2, expresses:

> *That he who reads may read it speedily*: interpreted this concerns the Teacher of Righteousness, to whom God made known all the mysteries of the words of His servants the Prophets

The writer of the commentary, unlike modern scholars, was not concerned with the original meaning of the biblical text, but solely with its significance for his own day. In 1QpHab

2:10–15, for example, the sixth-century BCE Chaldeans (or Babylonians) of Habakkuk 1:6 are equated with the Kittim or Romans of the first century BCE. Several other historical players in the late Second Temple period are likewise mentioned cryptically, most notably the Wicked Priest (probably Jonathan Maccabee) and the Liar (probably the Spouter of Lies or Scoffer of CD who apostatized from the sect). 1QpHab can, therefore, help in the reconstruction of the community's origins, especially when combined with the data supplied by CD. Helpful in this regard are other less well preserved commentaries (4QpHos, 1QpMic, 4QpPs). That on Nahum (4QpNah), in particular, refers to Antiochus IV and Demetrius III, as highlighted earlier.

Other sectarian compositions, such as 4QFlorilegium and 4QTestimonia, interpret a selection of diverse scriptural passages. 4QFlorilegium 1:14–16 illustrates this point:

> Explanation of *How blessed is the man who does not walk in the counsel of the wicked* (Ps. i,1). Interpreted, this saying [concerns] those who turn aside from the way [of the people] as it is written in the book of Isaiah the Prophet concerning the last days, *It came to pass that [the Lord turned me aside . . . from walking in the way of] this people* (Isa. viii, 11).

This kind of work culls verses from several biblical books to bolster its argument. In 4QFlorilegium, biblical statements about the righteous are reapplied to the sectarians, while the wicked are assumed analogous to outsiders. 4QTestimonia, on the other hand, interprets passages from Numbers and Deuteronomy more specifically in terms of a future prophetic figure and the two messianic characters who also feature in 1QS and CD.

III   *Hymns and Liturgies*

A third grouping of sectarian documents contains hymns, prayers and liturgies for private and communal usage. Because of their devotional nature, they communicate aspects of the sect's spirituality absent from other works. It is worth focusing on several examples.

The Hymns Scroll (1QH), a lengthy but damaged text, comprises an indeterminate number of poems thanking God for the knowledge and salvation granted the community. 1QH 10:14–16 is a representative sample:

> Blessed art Thou, O Lord,
>   God of mercy [and abundant] grace,
> for Thou hast made known [Thy wisdom to me
>   that I should recount] Thy marvellous deeds,
>   keeping silence neither by day nor [by night]!
> [For I have trusted] in Thy grace.
> In Thy great goodness,
>   and in [the multitude of Thy mercies] . . .

Designed for communal worship are multiple copies of the Shirot 'Olat ha-Shabbat (Songs of the Sabbath Sacrifice) retrieved from Caves 4 and 11 (4QShirShab[a–h] and 11QShirShab). The songs mention the heavenly Temple and the divine throne. They purport to reproduce the celestial worship of the first thirteen Sabbaths of the year, as 4QShirShab 20, ii, 21–22 shows:

> For the Mas[ter. Song of the holocaust of] the twelfth [S]abbath [on the twenty-first of the third month.]
>   [Praise the God of . . . w]onder, and exalt Him . . .
> The [cheru]bim prostrate themselves before Him and bless. As they rise, a whispered divine voice [is heard], and there is a roar of praise. When they drop their wings, there is a [whispere]d divine voice. The

> cherubim bless the image of the throne chariot above
> the firmament, [and] they praise [the majes]ty of the
> luminous firmament beneath His seat of glory.

'Holocaust' here is another term for sacrifice and the 'cherubim' are supernatural creatures, while the general imagery reflects Ezekiel 1 and 10. The community seems to have believed that, by employing these Songs, it could participate in the worship of heaven.

In order to shadow the celestial liturgy, an accurate calendar was required. Only recently available in full, copies of 4QCalendar A–F served that purpose by correlating three things: the solar calendar, the lunar calendar and the twenty-four priestly courses assigned duty in the Temple week-by-week. The end result does not make for exciting reading. But, as observed at the outset of this chapter, 4QCalendar C mentions in passing Shelamzion (Salome Alexandra) and Aemilius Scaurus (the first Roman governor of Syria).[39]

Finally, two messianic texts deserve brief mention. First, 1QSb, also known as Blessings and originally appended to 1QS, contains several benedictions to be uttered by the Guardian, one of the community's leaders, during the messianic age, as he addresses the different elements of the sect in turn: ordinary members, the Messiah of Aaron, the sons of Zadok and the Messiah of Israel. Second, the Messianic Apocalypse or 4QMessApoc is a poetic text which describes an anointed figure, as well as the healing and bodily resurrection that will accompany the advent of God's kingdom. Its importance lies in its reference to resurrection, a theme absent from other sectarian DSS, and in its combined themes of healing, resurrection and the Kingdom of God. These motifs, drawing in part on Isaiah 61:1, are also found in Luke 4:18.

IV   *Miscellaneous*

Some DSS do not fit into any of the above categories. Among them is the fragmentary 4QpapDoodles, which comprises random unintelligible doodles written on papyrus scraps. As for 4Q342–359, these documents consist of accounts, receipts and letters, although doubt has recently been cast on the Qumran origins of a number of them. It appears that some or all were actually retrieved from the Murabba'at or Nahal Hever vicinity and subsequently mixed up with material from the Qumran caves by antiquities dealers who had purchased them from the Bedouin.[40]

Rather more unusual is the Copper Scroll from Cave 3, also known as 3QTreasure. Inscribed on copper, it contains a list of riches hidden in sixty-four sites. Scholars disagree over whether its semi-cryptic account is fictional or literal and over the question of to whom the riches may have belonged. John Allegro, one of the original team of DSS researchers, embarked on an unofficial search for the Copper Scroll's riches in 1962, but came away empty-handed.

Yet more bizarre is what seems to be a horoscope in 4QCryptic. Not only is it penned in a mixture of Old Hebrew, Square Hebrew and Greek letters, but it also correlates a person's physical and spiritual characteristics with the position of the planets when he was born. 4QCryptic 2:5–6 reads:

> . . . his thighs are long and lean, and his toes are thin and long. He is of the second Column. His spirit consists of six (parts) in the House of Light and three in the Pit of Darkness. And this is his birthday on which he (is to be/was?) born: in the foot of the Bull. He will be meek. And his animal is the bull.

'Second Column' here may denote the second House, while the 'foot of the Bull' probably refers to the sun's location towards the bottom of the constellation Taurus. More significant is the assumption that the relative good (light) or evil (darkness) in a person was predetermined by the position of the stars at birth. The case cited constitutes that of a moderately good man.

Documents like 3QTreasure and 4QCryptic, although often fragmentary or difficult to understand for other reasons, add a touch of intrigue and colour to our perception of the nature of the DSS. The recently released 4QBrontologion, predicting marvels and disasters by interpreting the significance of thunder on a given day of the month, does likewise. Despite their real value, however, it should be made clear that such texts do not alter scholars' overall estimation of the collection.

AN ESSENE COMMUNITY AT QUMRAN

So far, having first seen that they probably emanated from a group linked to the Essenes described by Philo, Josephus and Pliny, we have briefly surveyed some of the main sectarian DSS – although a few other documents will crop up in subsequent chapters. If we add to this equation our earlier review of the late Second Temple period, as well as the chronological framework confirmed by carbon dating, palaeography and archaeology, then two further tasks demand our attention. First, it is possible to work out the main contours of the sect's origins and history. Second, we can summarize its practices and beliefs.

I *Qumran Origins and History*

Even though the Qumran caves yielded no historical document in the modern academic sense, a few works do supply us with some historical reminiscences, as observed already. Such data, given our general knowledge of Second Temple times, allow a reconstruction of the circumstances of the birth and growth of the Qumran community. CD 1:3–12 is a good place to begin:[41]

> [3]For when they were unfaithful and forsook Him, He hid His face from Israel and His Sanctuary [4]and delivered them up to the sword. But remembering the Covenant of the forefathers, He left a remnant [5]to Israel and did not deliver it up to be destroyed. And in the age of wrath, three hundred [6]and ninety years after He had delivered them into the hands of King Nebuchadnezzar of Babylon, [7]He visited them, and He caused a plant root to spring from Israel and Aaron to inherit [8]His Land and to prosper on the good things of His earth. And they perceived their iniquity and recognised that [9-10]they were guilty men, yet for twenty years they were like blind men groping for the way.
>
> And God observed their deeds, that they sought Him with a whole heart, [11]and He raised for them a Teacher of Righteousness to guide them in the way of His heart. And he made known [12]to the latter generations that which God had done to the latter generation, the congregation of traitors, to those who departed from the way.

The foundational events described here confirm that the group behind the sectarian DSS formed under the Teacher of Righteousness in the second century BCE. The 'three hundred and ninety' and 'twenty' years from Nebuchadnezzar's capture of Jerusalem, bringing us to 177 BCE, should be taken with a pinch of salt, since we know from Josephus and others that Second Temple Jews were unsure about the exact length of the Babylonian exile. The figures are probably symbolic, moreover, for 'three hundred and ninety' comes from Ezekiel 4:5, while 'twenty' represents half a generation.

In any case, CD 1:8–10 envisages a penitential movement struggling to seek God's will, whose members have been identified by many scholars as the 'Hasideans' of 1 Maccabees 2:42, active in the 160s BCE. Into this situation, according to CD 1:11–12, entered the Teacher of Righteousness. He became the group's leader and taught them God's ways, explaining, perhaps, that Antiochus IV's persecution of Judaism was divine retribution for unfaithfulness.

The Teacher of Righteousness also features prominently in 1QpHab, as does his main opponent, the Wicked Priest. The actual identity of the former remains elusive.[42] But most experts equate the latter with Jonathan Maccabee and highlight 1QpHab 8:3–12:

> *Moreover, the arrogant man seizes wealth without halting. He widens his gullet like Hell and like Death he has never enough. All the nations are gathered to him and all the peoples are assembled to him. Will they not all of them taunt him and jeer at him saying, 'Woe to him who amasses that which is not his! How long will he load himself up with pledges?'* (ii, 5–6).

> Interpreted, this concerns the Wicked Priest who was called by the name of truth when he first arose. But when he ruled over Israel his heart became proud, and he forsook God and betrayed the precepts for the sake of riches. He robbed and amassed the riches of the men of violence who rebelled against God, and he took the wealth of the peoples, heaping sinful iniquity upon himself.

The fall of the Wicked Priest from grace here matches what must have been the reversal in many people's estimation of

Jonathan Maccabee after his assumption of the High Priesthood in 152 BCE. As pointed out earlier, only the line of Zadok was supposed to supply High Priests. The fact that several sectarian DSS stress the Zadokite credentials of the Qumran community strongly suggests that it included dissidents offended by Jonathan Maccabee's acceptance of pontifical office, including a number of Zadokite priests. Other elements in 1QpHab's description of the Wicked Priest, moreover, tally with the career of Jonathan Maccabee: he built up Jerusalem, was victorious in battle, only to be captured and killed by a foreigner.[43]

With the release of 4QMMT in 1991, it now seems that this was only one element provoking discontent. Equally important were other disputes over the interpretation of the Torah in matters relating to the calendar, ritual purity and marriage. Disagreements over such contentious issues, alongside Jonathan Maccabee's elevation as High Priest, seem to have led the group headed by the Teacher of Righteousness to make a definitive break. Despite the early conciliatory tone evident in 4QMMT, the Wicked Priest is said to have sought the death of the Teacher in 4QpPs 4:8–9, while 1QpHab 11:2–8 records an attack by the former on the latter at his 'place of exile', presumably Qumran.

A move to Qumran by the Teacher of Righteousness in the decades following Jonathan Maccabee's accession as High Priest in 152 BCE tallies with the archaeological evidence gleaned from the site. 1QS 8:12–16, one of the oldest parts of the document, fits such a reconstruction:

> And when these become members of the Community in Israel according to all these rules, they shall separate from the habitation of unjust men and shall go into the wilderness to prepare there the way of Him; as it is written, *Prepare in the wilderness the way of . . . , make*

straight in the desert a path for our God (Isa. xl,3). This (path) is the study of the Law which He commanded by the hand of Moses, that they may do according to all that has been revealed from age to age, and as the Prophets have revealed by His Holy Spirit.

As predicted by the prophet Isaiah, the Teacher and his followers absconded to Qumran, also known cryptically as 'Damascus' in CD 6:5. There, they lived according to their strict interpretation of the Law and awaited God's intervention to end the current evil age.

Earlier in the chapter, we concluded that the 'furious young lion' in 4QpNah 1:6–7 describes Alexander Jannaeus who executed eight hundred Pharisees in 88 BCE.[44] A careful reading of this and other passages reveals further information about the sect's relations with outsiders. The author refers to the Pharisees as 'those who seek smooth things' because of what he viewed as their less-than-stringent obedience to the Law. The same group is also called 'Ephraim', a biblical name which, along with Manasseh, denotes one of the apostate northern tribes of Israel before the exile. Not surprisingly, the insult 'Manasseh' is employed in 4QpNah 2:1–3:9 and 4QpPs 1–10, 2:18–20 of another despised group which, since it includes 'mighty men' and 'honourable men', is best identified as the Sadducees.

As well as the 'furious young lion', Jannaeus is dubbed the 'last priest' in 4QpHos 2:2–3. Presumably, the 'last priests of Jerusalem' in 1QpHab 9:4 denote other members of the Hasmonean dynasty. They would soon be punished for their wickedness, believed the author, by the Kittim. These Kittim are certainly the Romans, viewed throughout 1QpHab as God's instruments for the implementation of justice. However, by the time 1QM and 4QRule of War were composed in the late first century BCE or early first century CE, the Romans were evaluated rather differently. Now that they were in control of Palestine, they were vilified as the arch-enemies of God who would themselves be defeated in the cosmic battle precipitating the advent of God's kingdom.

Unfortunately, even though 1QM was probably composed in the first century CE, neither it nor other sectarian documents tell us anything about individuals inside or outside the community during Phase II. All we know is that the sect's occupation of Khirbet Qumran ended with the advent of the Roman armies in the region. They put the community to flight, subsequently using Khirbet Qumran themselves as an outpost. Fortunately for us, the members of the sect abandoned their books to posterity, although some of the surrounding caves may already have been in use for library purposes.[45]

This outline of the history of the Qumran community represents a scholarly consensus the basic components of which had taken shape by the 1960s.[46] During the 1970s and 1980s, however, a number of scholars began to question some of its constituent elements. Yet their dissent from the dominant consensus should not be exaggerated. Essentially, a few experts have argued that the community at Qumran was not the headquarters of the Essene sect described by the classical sources but the home of a splinter group which seceded from the broad Essene movement of Philo and Josephus. The main evidence adduced in favour of such a theory is CD 1:3–12, cited above. This passage, so the argument goes, assumes a pious 'remnant' existed soon after Nebuchadnezzar's destruction of Jerusalem but long before the rise of the 'root of planting' three hundred and ninety years later and the 'Teacher of Righteousness' twenty years later still.

Philip Davies of the University of Sheffield, for example, has proposed that CD 1:3–5 describes a group which claimed an exilic origin in the sixth century BCE.[47] The members of that movement, he argues, were the Essenes of Philo and Josephus, whereas the Teacher of Righteousness, mentioned in CD 1:11–12 and other sectarian DSS, provoked a schism and parted company with these Essenes in the mid-second century BCE. Two scholars in the Netherlands, F. García Martínez and A. S. van der Woude of Groningen University, have put forward a similar case.[48] They have proposed that the Essenes of the classical sources already existed in Judaea as a broad movement during the late third and early second century BCE. In the 160s and 150s BCE, a dispute arose within it, prompting a breakaway faction to reject its Essene parent group and set up camp on its own at Qumran.

Both views are possible alternative reconstructions of the origins and identity of the community behind the DSS and contain elements that are proving increasingly attractive to a variety of experts in the field. Because they continue to posit a strong link between the community at Qumran and the Essenes, however, they should be classed as variants of the Essene hypothesis.

II   *Qumran Practice and Belief*

The sectarian DSS tend not to state explicitly the community's beliefs. This omission is hardly surprising, for Jews have rarely felt the need to formulate a systematic theology, while even Christians only began to do so from the third century CE. On the basis of its writings, nevertheless, it is possible to determine the sect's basic theological stance and its mode of behaviour. Of course, many elements are taken straight from the Bible or else constitute post-biblical developments in practice and belief shared by all Second Temple Jews. Others constitute more peculiar features, distinctive of the Qumran community.

One such distinctive characteristic is the determinism evident in a variety of sectarian compositions, as noted earlier. Even Satan, who sometimes tricks the sectarians into sin, is mysteriously under God's control as part of the divine plan, according to 1QS 3:21–24:

> The Angel of Darkness leads all the children of righteousness astray, and until his end, all their sin, iniquities, wickedness, and all their unlawful deeds are caused by his dominion in accordance with the mysteries of God.

Inherent within this predestined order are 'the way of light' and 'the way of darkness'. In other words, two opposing forces – good and evil – make their influence felt throughout the universe, according to the spiritual instruction about the 'two spirits' in 1QS 4:15–17:

> The nature of all the children of men is ruled by these (two spirits), and during their life all the hosts of men have a portion of their divisions and walk in (both) their ways. And the whole reward for their deeds shall be, for everlasting ages, according to whether each man's portion in their two divisions is great or small. For God has established the spirits in equal measure until the final age, and has set everlasting hatred between their divisions.

As 1QM makes clear, the conflict between the two spirits rages in the angelic realm as much as between and within human beings. Ultimately, only God's intervention will ensure the victory of good and vindicate the sect.

Meanwhile, the sectarians, like other Jews, believed God was more subtly involved in human affairs. Abraham had been singled out for special blessing and, most importantly, God had revealed the Torah to his descendants, the people of Israel, through Moses on Mount Sinai. After the Babylonian exile, God ensured the survival of a faithful remnant and, as the continuation of that remnant, the Qumran community claimed its special status as the true Israel. Like biblical Israel, it had priestly members (called Aaron) and lay persons (referred to as Israel), while, for purposes of war, the laity were subdivided into Thousands, Hundreds, Fifties and Tens (1QS 2:21 and CD 13:1–2).

The sect also had its own additional layers of organization, although divergences suggest that changes took place over time. In early passages, for example, the whole community seems to have been the final authority, while in later documents the sons of Zadok wield ultimate power. One feasible explanation for this difference is that, during its formative years, the movement was run on democratic lines, with the whole Congregation acting as the final authority; this arrangement seems to be reflected in an early edition of the Community Rule retrieved from Cave 4 in the shape of 4QS^{b,d}. Soon afterwards, perhaps with the advent of the Teacher of Righteousness described in CD 1:11–12, a priestly Zadokite elite emerged to lead the sect, as appears to be assumed in 1QS, the later and fuller edition of the Community Rule.

On a day-to-day level, the Guardian or Master was in control, together with his companion the Bursar and the Council of the Community. In 1QS 6:8–9, however, the latter is the whole sect, whereas in 1QS 8:1–4 the Council consists of twelve lay and three priestly members. These arrangements pertained in any case to the Qumran headquarters, while the provisions for the secondary 'camps' were somewhat different. Each camp was headed by a lesser Guardian who was assisted by a tribunal of judges made up of six lay and four priestly members. Yet, the whole movement seems to have gathered once a year under the principal Guardian of 1QS, the 'guardian of all the camps' (CD 14:3–6). The community's covenant with God was renewed and members were ranked in accord with their spiritual progress, as 1QS 2:19–25 seems to describe:

> Thus shall they do, year by year, for as long as the dominion of Satan endures. The Priests shall enter first, ranked after one another according to the perfection of their spirit; then the Levites; and thirdly, all the people . . . in their Thousands, Hundreds, Fifties, and Tens . . . No man shall move down from his place nor move up from his allotted position. For according to the holy design, they shall all of them be in a Community of truth and virtuous humility, of lovingkindness and good intent . . . and (they shall all of them be) sons of the everlasting Company.

The remainder of 1QS 1:16–3:12 shows that new members were admitted at this time and others expelled. According to 4QD[e], the relevant gathering took place in the 'third month', probably during the Feast of Tabernacles in the autumn. It is this yearly attendance at the Feast by women and children from the secondary 'camps' which may account for the limited number of female and child skeletons excavated from the Qumran cemetery; it seems likely that, over a period of two hundred years, some will inevitably have died during their visit and been laid to rest among the bodily remains of the primary community which was otherwise exclusively male.

For people outside the sect, no knowledge of God was possible, and here the contribution of the Teacher of Righteousness was vital. 1QpHab maintains that he and his successors possessed a unique ability to interpret the Torah and other scriptures for their own times. Such legal concerns explain the sect's zealous devotion to the Law and the stipulation in 1QS 8:21–23 that any breach of it should result in expulsion:

> Every man who enters the Council of Holiness . . . who deliberately or through negligence transgresses one word of the Law of Moses, on any point whatever,

97

> shall be expelled from the Council of the Community
> and shall return no more . . .

In addition, the sect derived from the Torah fresh interpretations of existing laws, along with new rules it thought had been hidden in the text specially for the last days. This exegetical process lies behind the strict Sabbath and purity laws in CD and 4QMMT, as well as the regulations governing community life in 1QS and CD. Another particularly distinctive feature was the calendar. It differed from the lunar system employed in the Jerusalem Temple by combining both solar and lunar characteristics. This divergence explains how, according to 1QpHab 11:3–8, the Teacher could have been attacked on the Day of Atonement:

> *Woe to him who causes his neighbours to drink; who pours out his venom to make them drunk that he may gaze on their feasts* (ii, 15).
>
> Interpreted, this concerns the Wicked Priest who pursued the Teacher of Righteousness to the house of his exile that he might confuse him with his venomous fury. And at the time appointed for rest, for the Day of Atonement, he appeared before them to confuse them, and to cause them to stumble on the Day of Fasting, their Sabbath of repose.

The Wicked Priest did not rest because for outsiders, unlike the Qumran community, the date in question was not the real Day of Atonement.

The insight claimed by the Teacher also had implications for the interpretation of scripture outside the Torah. Indeed, it was believed that a correct understanding of biblical books like Isaiah or Habakkuk showed that the 'latter days' or 'age of wickedness' had arrived. In other words, the sect believed it was living in the final phase of world history, during which it was the sole locus of truth and divine favour; outside was sin and darkness. This conviction explains the urgent tone of many sectarian documents, as well as the polemic aimed at Jews outside. According to 1QM, this state of affairs would culminate in a final forty-year battle. The community awaited the advent of at least two special figures, although its beliefs in this regard seem to have evolved over time.

The earliest strand is that which envisages the coming of a Priest-Messiah only, as in 4QpPs 3:15 and CD 6:11. Such an expectation is entirely understandable, given the scriptural promises made to the priesthood and the fact that the Hebrew term *mashiach*, 'anointed (one)', could evoke the anointing of the High Priest as much as the anointing of the Davidic king. Nevertheless, perhaps in order to compete with the stress on the latter prominent in some other Jewish circles, those responsible for the DSS seem subsequently to have conjoined the notion of an anointed High Priest with that of a Davidic Messiah. This can be seen in CD 20:1, with its reference to the 'coming of the Messiah out of Aaron and Israel'. The next stage was a belief in the arrival of two separate figures – a Priest-Messiah or 'Messiah of Aaron' and a Davidic Messiah or 'Messiah of Israel', with the latter subordinate to the former. This scenario is described in 1QS 9:11, with the expectation of 'the Messiahs of Aaron and Israel', and, as we saw earlier, especially in 1QSa. Ample scriptural warrant exists for this combination in the post-exilic books of Haggai and Zechariah 1–8.[49] Staying with 1QS 9:11, it also refers to the advent of 'the prophet', whom some scholars identify as a third messianic figure.[50] It seems, therefore, that the sect's formulations of messianic hope reflect the fact that in the Bible both priests and kings and, occasionally, prophets could be anointed.

WHAT ABOUT THE PHARISEES, SADDUCEES AND ZEALOTS?

It should be clear by now that a good case can be made for attributing an Essene identity to the community at Qumran. The strength of the evidence adduced lies in its cumulative force. Nevertheless, during the 1950s and 1960s other identifications were proposed, based on apparent links between the sectarian DSS and what is known of the Sadducees, Pharisees and Zealots. It is worth commenting briefly on three alternative theories.

First, let us consider the Sadducees. The only explicit information we possess about the Sadducees comes from two sources written by non-Sadducees – the New Testament and Josephus. Both suggest that the Sadducees were closely connected to Jerusalem's leading aristocratic and priestly families in the last two hundred years of the Second Temple period. The name itself probably derives from Zadok, the priest from the days of King David whose line was supposed to supply the High Priests of Second Temple times.[51] In any case, the Sadducees were wealthy and influential. Understandably, therefore, their favour was courted by all the leaders of Judaea from the Hasmoneans to the Roman procurators. Only Salome Alexandra, on the advice of her husband, seems to have allied herself with the Pharisees in view of their widespread popularity.

Even this briefest of outlines makes it clear that genuine links exist between the Sadducees and the community reflected in the sectarian DSS. Most noticeable is the emphasis placed by both on the priesthood, especially the Zadok line. As we shall see in Chapter 6, there are also some real parallels when it comes to interpretation of the laws in the Pentateuch. But there the similarities end. The Sadducees come across as part of a rich ruling elite, centred on Jerusalem and its Temple and happy with the status quo. As for the Qumran community, on the other hand, a tone of dissatisfaction with the current state of affairs permeates writings like 1QS, CD, and 1QpHab, as we have learned. In contrast to the Sadducees, moreover, 11QT and 1QM have an expectation that the present order, especially the Temple and its priesthood, will soon be swept away and replaced by a superior system in line with God's will. More specifically still, the sectarian DSS betray a belief in angels (4QShirShab, 11QMelch) and the resurrection of the dead (4QMessApoc). Since Josephus informs us that the Sadducees rejected both notions, any attempt to identify the Qumran sect as Sadducean must ultimately fail.[52]

Might it be possible to argue instead that the Pharisees lie behind the Qumran manuscripts? To piece together a picture of the Pharisees, we are dependent on the New Testament, Josephus and later Rabbinic literature written after 70 CE.[53] The Pharisees were essentially a group of pious Jews who, although predominantly lay, sought to organize their lives as though they were priests subject to the purity rules of the Temple. Consequently, they were fastidious when it came to applying the Torah's commands about diet and purity; this in turn resulted in their reputation as experts in Bible interpretation. As remarked earlier, the Pharisees seem to have been highly regarded by the ordinary people, even though they numbered only about six thousand. They may have formed fellowships, entry into which was permitted after a flexible trial period. As for the name Pharisee, derived from the Hebrew verb *parash* ('to separate'), it may originally have been applied as a nickname by outsiders who noticed the group's segregation for the purposes of ritual purity.

There are some obvious similarities between the Pharisees and the group behind the sectarian DSS.[54] Both were concerned with ritual purity and had a special interest in biblical interpretation. Likewise, each group had a training period before membership was permitted. These parallels are out-weighed by differences, however. Despite their common zeal for ritual purity, the Qumran sect's concern stemmed from the special place allotted to the Zadokite priests in its midst, while the Pharisees were essentially a lay party. The Pharisees' separation, moreover, was not as strict as that envisaged by the sectarian DSS, nor did it extend to keeping its teachings secret. Notwithstanding some real overlaps, therefore, it is highly unlikely that those responsible for the sectarian DSS were Pharisees. On the contrary, we concluded in the last section that the insulting nicknames 'Ephraim' and 'Manasseh' in 4QpNah and 4QpPs refer to the Pharisees and Sadducees, respectively, as opponents outside the sect.

Another group of Second Temple Jews has been put forward as a third possible candidate for the community at Qumran – the Zealots.[55] Unfortunately, gleaning objective data about them from Josephus, our major source, is problematic. Josephus makes plain his loathing for the Zealots, blaming them almost entirely for the First Revolt against Rome. Given his own acknowledged involvement in that Revolt, his representation of the Zealots should not be taken at face value. Nevertheless, it is possible to build up a general picture. Accordingly, the label Zealot is best employed as an umbrella term denoting a variety of individuals and their followers, all of whom were united by their zeal for an independent Jewish state. The origins of the movement can be traced to the transformation of Judaea and Samaria into a Roman province in 6 CE. This development necessitated a census of the people, an imposition which outraged one Judas the Galilean and a Pharisee called Zadok. Although disturbances at the time were put down, members of Judas' family remained prominent in the decades to follow in a loose coalition of Zealots – including the sicarii, men armed with a dagger or *sica*, active in the 60s CE – who sought freedom for the Jews under the rule of God alone.

At first sight, several Zealot features might suggest that the Qumran sect was part of their movement.[56] 1QM's expectation of a final cosmic battle, with the Romans as the arch-enemies, seems to point in this direction, as does the presence of a copy of 4QShirShab at Masada, a definite Zealot outpost. Other explanations for the latter are preferable. It is possible, for example, that members of the Qumran sect fled to Masada in desperation as the Roman armies loomed large on the horizon, taking a handful of documents with them. A more significant circumstance further militates against a direct association between those at Qumran and the Zealots. Although the latter arose in the first century CE, the Qumran site had by then been in use for over one hundred years. It is this factor, coupled with allusions in the sectarian documents to people and events in the first and second centuries BCE, which makes it difficult to give credence to the notion that Qumran was a Zealot community.

The above outline has shown that alternative proposals for the identity of the community at Qumran are unlikely to be correct. Nonetheless, we shall see in Chapter 6 that their weakness has not prevented renewed efforts to resurrect some of them in recent times. For now, it is worth reaffirming that, given both the general and specific connections between the sectarian DSS and the accounts of Philo, Josephus and Pliny, a form of Essene hypothesis seems inescapable.

THE DEAD SEA SCROLLS AND THE ESSENES

This chapter has sought to demonstrate that the sectarian DSS reflect a religious community which was Essene or, at least, had seceded from an Essene parent group. Our reconstruction of the sect's origins and history, as well as its practices and beliefs, was far from exhaustive. Several elements taken for granted by most scholars since the 1960s have been questioned or reformulated in recent years. We observed, for example, that a number of scholars now view the Qumran community as an Essene splinter group.[57] Nevertheless, by fitting most of the pieces of the jigsaw, as it were, into a broad coherent whole, some form of Essene hypothesis remains the best option. We have seen that, while other theories can conjure up various alternative linkages between individual items, they are unable to account for the totality of the evidence in the same way.

In sum, members of the Qumran community followed a distinctive interpretation of the Torah and organizational structure, believing their sect to be the sole repository of divine truth. The Teacher of Righteousness, the inspired founder of the group in the second century BCE, had a special place in the affections of its members, while among subsequent leaders, the priests, notably the sons of Zadok, were prominent. Jews outside were, in contrast, held in contempt for their rejection of the sect's teachings and resultant legal bankruptcy, although they would have a chance to mend their ways during the final battle between good and evil.

CHAPTER 4

The Dead Sea Scrolls
and Judaism

THE NATURE OF THE EVIDENCE

The sectarian DSS have given us a glimpse into the life of a religious party with Essene connections which flourished in the last two centuries BCE and the first century CE. We can now turn our attention to the wider world of late Second Temple Judaism by placing the scrolls alongside other relevant literature – late biblical material, Apocrypha and Pseudepigrapha, Philo and Josephus, the New Testament and Rabbinic writings. Afterwards, for the sake of completeness, it will be worthwhile explaining how Judaism developed in the centuries following the destruction of the Temple in 70 CE. Then, in the last section of this chapter, we shall briefly consider what impact the DSS might have on Judaism in the modern world.

Beginning with Judaism in Second Temple times, it is important to realize that, in contrast to the direct nature of the Qumran evidence, all other available sources are marred by limitations of one sort or another. For example, both the authorship and date of many books from the Bible, Apocrypha and Pseudepigrapha remain unclear. It is difficult to be sure, therefore, about the degree to which the perspective of, say, Daniel or Jubilees was commonplace or marginal. As for the New Testament, although it has long been drawn on for an impression of what Judaism was like in the time of Jesus, we noted earlier that academic study has shown many New Testament books were compiled after 70 CE. This applies especially to a chapter in the Gospels such as Matthew 24 which lambasts the Pharisees for their hypocrisy. Rather than an objective description, this passage probably reflects rivalry between Jews and Christians in the last quarter of the first century CE.

Caution is also required when reading Josephus. He lived from 37 CE until around 100 CE and spent the first half of his life in Jerusalem. Born into a well-to-do priestly family, Josephus was an educated man who doubtless led a relatively comfortable existence, although it probably had its share of trials and tribulations. One such occasion may have been his visit to Rome at the age of twenty-seven to seek the release of some Jewish prisoners in 64 CE, just two years before the outbreak of the First Revolt. Yet this event suggests Josephus was a moderate who, though proud of his Jewish heritage, was more or less content with the status quo of Roman rule in Palestine.

After 70 CE, in fact, Josephus settled in Rome as a favourite of the emperors Vespasian and Titus.[1] Even though he had been a general stationed in Galilee during the Revolt, he managed to ingratiate himself with the enemy after capture, apparently predicting correctly that the general in charge of the Roman army, Vespasian, would soon become emperor. From the imperial capital, he subsequently wrote four works: *Jewish War*, *Jewish Antiquities*, the *Life* and *Against Apion*.[2] In these writings, Josephus tried to show a wide Jewish–Gentile audience that, notwithstanding the war with Rome, the Jews were a peace-loving nation and Judaism a noble religion. He also sought to demonstrate that both he and the Romans had behaved impeccably during the First Revolt, which was largely the fault of a small band of rebels. Unfortunately, both these aims, as well as Josephus' mixed readership, occasioned considerable, if sporadic, oversimplification and idealization, as we have seen in relation to the Essenes already. Such tendencies are so pronounced in his accounts of the First Revolt as to obfuscate its precise causes – not to mention Josephus' true colours before switching to the Roman side after his imprisonment.[3]

As for Jewish literature composed after 70 CE, it too has its own agenda. Among other things, the rabbis who compiled the Mishnah (*circa* 200 CE) and the Talmud (around 550 CE) were at pains to establish themselves as the heirs of the Pharisees from the Second Temple period. Their aim in so doing was to legitimize the religious system they developed afterwards, as well as their own authoritative place within it. Consequently, historians are reluctant to take at face value the elevated position attributed to the Pharisees in Rabbinic literature, as we shall see later.

Because of such limitations, the sources available before the discovery of the DSS provide neither a straightforward general description of Second Temple Judaism nor a first-hand account of specific religious parties. By using the sectarian documents as a corrective, however, and combining their evidence with that of the other sources, we can reconstruct some of the major features of Judaism in Second Temple times.

JUDAISM OR JUDAISMS?

Paradoxically, the main inference to be drawn is the impossibility of reducing Second Temple Judaism to a single definition. Apart from anything else, too many gaps remain in the evidence, while what information we do have highlights considerable divergence in practice and belief among the religious groups we have thus far surveyed. Each party doubtless believed its own outlook was superior, especially the community at Qumran which judged all outsiders to be apostate. Nevertheless, as historians, we are not in a position arbitrarily to deem one perspective a truer representation of Judaism than any other. More neutral is the suggestion that each group embodied a particular formulation of what, in its view, constituted being a good Jew amid the complex circumstances of the day. In other words, the distinctive characteristics of each community were alternative responses to this basic question – formulated according to the needs and predilections of the group concerned, as well as the particular set of religious traditions that happened to be available in a given time and place.

This characterization of Jewish practice and belief has led some scholars to speak of 'Judaisms' in the plural rather than a single 'Judaism'.[4] Indeed, the array of Jewish identities current in the Second Temple period makes this an attractive proposition, for, apart from the Pharisees, Sadducees and Essenes, we should not forget about the Zealots and the early Christians. Even the Samaritans could be included in the list because, apart from their preference for a Temple in Gerizim rather than Jerusalem, their distinguishing features were probably no greater than those marking out the other Jewish parties.[5]

This overwhelming impression of diversity is further exacerbated when we consider Jews in the Diaspora or Dispersion – that is, Jews living outside Palestine. Although they have not featured in our enquiry so far, a sizeable Jewish Diaspora evolved in the late Second Temple period, as war, commerce or simple curiosity drove Jews abroad. They were spread over too wide an area to form a distinct religious party. Nevertheless, Diaspora Judaism had a greater tendency to absorb the ideas and customs of the surrounding non-Jewish world. Although this susceptibility should not be exaggerated, Jews in, say, Alexandria, Athens or Rome, were inclined to assimilate towards Gentile culture more thoroughly than those living in Palestine. Philo, an older contemporary of Josephus who lived between 15 BCE and 50 CE, is an interesting example. Writing from Alexandria in Egypt, he set out to synthesize Jewish and Greek thought. A similar trait is evident in the book of Wisdom from the Apocrypha.[6] Like Philo, it portrays the Jewish hope of life after death in the Greek guise of the soul's immortality, rejecting the notion of a bodily resurrection favoured in Palestine.

To sum up so far, the religious parties and tendencies we have listed might well be described as a collection of Judaisms. Notwithstanding their overlaps in practice and belief, the serious divergences which existed between them meant that each competed with the others for the attention of Second Temple Jews. We have already observed that the sectarian DSS employed insulting nicknames (like the 'Seekers of Smooth Things' or 'Ephraim') for the adherents of other parties, while the same sort of rivalry comes across in Acts 23:6–10, where Paul is pictured taking advantage of the doctrinal disputes between the Pharisees and Sadducees. In such circumstances, no one party can be said to have constituted a normative or 'orthodox' Judaism, and so the claims of Rabbinic literature in that regard are inaccurate. The rabbis' assumption that the Pharisees had represented a kind of mainstream Judaism was, therefore, an anachronistic projection from their own day. Pharisaic piety cannot be equated with the religion of ordinary people in the last two centuries BCE or the first century CE, especially if the Pharisees, despite their popularity with the masses, numbered only some six thousand, as Josephus states. On the other hand, the Sadducees of the Temple establishment, as a small wealthy elite, can hardly have been representative either. Nor have we any reason to believe that the closely-guarded practices and beliefs of the Essenes were adopted by Jews outside their own membership.

Yet this evidence for diversity might not be the whole story. We have already observed that the membership of the Pharisees, Sadducees and Essenes numbered no more than several thousand each. Such figures show that, even when combined, they could have accounted for no more than a minority of the Jewish population. Consequently, there must have been large numbers who did not belong to any religious party, especially if we include Diaspora Jews in the picture.[7] So, what about the ordinary masses of Jewish men, women and children? It is here that it may still make sense to return to the singular and speak of a 'common Judaism'.[8] In other words, setting to one side the distinctive elements of the named religious parties, the average Jew in Second Temple times probably adhered to a basic core of practices and beliefs held in common. These had to do with God, with Israel as both land and people, with the Temple in Jerusalem, and, of course, with the Torah as God's ultimate revelation. Since it is likely that these elements constituted four common denominators among all Jews, it is worth saying a few words about the first three, while the Law will receive fuller attention in the next section.

Underlying all Jewish identities in the Second Temple period was a basic belief in the existence of the God of the Jews. Indeed, the Jews were renowned for their monotheistic worship of God without the use of images, unlike other religious cults in the Greek and Roman world. Not surprisingly, just how this Deity was envisaged could vary considerably. The picture of God that comes across from the sectarian DSS, for instance, might seem distant from Philo's concept which depends on Greek philosophy as much as on traditional Judaism. Even so, the adherents of both would have assumed their Deity was the same as the God who had called Abraham, revealed the Law to Moses, controlled the fate of ancient Israel and Judah, and still guided their descendants, the Jews. Beyond such essential basics, most Jews found it unnecessary to speculate further about God's attributes in the way later generations of Christians and, eventually, Jews would do. Alongside an elementary belief in God, however, the special status of the people of Israel was another indispensable foundation of Judaism.

Primarily, Israel was the people of God in the biblical period, so called after one of Abraham's grandsons, Jacob, who was himself renamed Israel (Genesis 32:28). According to the biblical story, his sons became twelve great tribes who settled in the land which also became known as Israel. Eventually, only the tribe of Judah survived intact and, as we explained in Chapter 1, Second Temple Jews believed they were its descendants. They held, in addition, that their relationship with God remained special, just as their ancestors' had been. Hand in hand with that belief went the unique status of the land inhabited by the Israelites of old and their heirs the Jews. Consequently, all Second Temple Jews would have felt a special bond with the land of Israel – Judaea, Samaria and Galilee – whether they happened to live in it or not. This link between land and people was one of the driving forces behind Hasmonean independence, as well as the First Revolt against Rome. It also remained an important factor when the traditional Jewish homeland was under foreign domination. During the Roman occupation, for instance, Jews from all over the world came on pilgrimage to major religious festivals like the Passover, the Feast of Weeks and the Feast of Tabernacles.[9] Such devotion is reflected in Acts 2:9–11, where the place-names listed show that Jews gathered in Jerusalem from far and wide on such occasions.

Of course, the Temple was the focal point of religious activity at such times, since it was thought to be the special locus of God's presence in the land among his people. To safeguard its sanctity, God had ordained a priesthood to perform ritual and sacrifice in accord with his will. Only they were allowed into the Temple's most hallowed parts, while the High Priest alone was permitted to enter the Holy of Holies at its heart once a year on the Day of Atonement. As for ordinary Jews, several sources take it for granted that they paid the Temple tax, a fixed sum which, following the injunctions in Exodus 30:11–16 and Nehemiah 10:32, was paid annually by all adult males for the upkeep of the Temple.[10] So widespread was adherence to this command, even among Jews in the Diaspora, that the Romans required the tax to be redirected to the temple of Jupiter in Rome after the defeat of the First Revolt in 70 CE.[11]

LAW AND APOCALYPTIC

I *The Role of the Law*

All Jews in our period would have accepted a fourth common denominator: rules regarding worship, the Temple and its priesthood, and a lot more besides, had been revealed by God in the Torah or Law of Moses. Although the brevity of many of its commandments necessitated interpretation, it nevertheless provided a kind of blueprint for Jewish life. Those unfamiliar with its legal tradition find this essential aspect of Judaism difficult to grasp. Here, therefore, we shall elaborate on the place of the Torah in Second Temple Judaism, before turning to more speculative doctrinal matters.

We have observed already that Judaism, like most religions in the ancient world, incorporated an elaborate system of worship and sacrifice focused on a central sanctuary, the Temple in Jerusalem, whose priesthood was regulated by the rules in the Pentateuch. Unusually, however, the Torah also extended its influence into every aspect of ordinary Jewish life. Being a good Jew was primarily about living according to God's will as revealed in the Law. To that extent, Judaism in Second

Temple times and beyond can be described as legalistic – concerned, that is, with obeying God's laws.

When understood on its own terms, Jewish legalism has a driving-force which should not be misconstrued as petty or burdensome. The second-century BCE text Ecclesiasticus serves as a good illustration. In chapter 24, praise is heaped upon divine Wisdom, personified as God's helper when the world was created. In Ecclesiasticus 24:23, the writer makes an important connection:

> All this is the book of the covenant of the Most High God,
>   the law that Moses commanded us
>   as an inheritance for the congregations of Jacob.

The very Wisdom of God is here said to be embodied in the Law of Moses. The only adequate response, naturally, is to follow its decrees to the letter, without any artificial distinction between ritual and ethical commandments. Indeed, all aspects of human life prescribed in the Torah – whether worshipping God, loving one's neighbour, punishing the murderer, offering sacrifice, or tithing grain – form one seamless whole. From within such an outlook, obedience to the Torah can only result in blessing for both the community and the individual, whereas disobedience brings disaster.

All the evidence suggests that Jews in the late Second Temple period accepted the divine origin of the Torah and kept most of its prescriptions most of the time. This conclusion is borne out by a number of non-Jewish writers who commented on certain well-known features of Jewish life.[12] The third-century CE Roman historian, Cassius Dio, for example, remarked on Jewish observance of the Sabbath at the time of Pompey's conquest of Jerusalem in 63 BCE:[13]

> For it [the Temple] was on high ground and was forti-
> fied by a wall of its own, and if they [the Jerusalemites]

had continued defending it on all days alike, he [Pompey] could not have got possession of it. As it was, they made an exception of what are called the days of Saturn [the Sabbath], and by doing no work at all on those days afforded the Romans an opportunity in this interval to batter down the wall.

In addition to the Sabbath, several other distinctive features of Judaism stood out: imageless worship of the one true God, circumcision of male children, abstention from pork and other dietary regulations, and purity rules to guard against ritual uncleanness.[14] The last could be transmitted via corpses or bodily emissions and, although not necessarily entailing any sin, required ritual washing to restore a state of cleanness. Priests serving in the Temple had to be particularly attentive to purity rules.

There can be little doubt that the bulk of the Jewish population was concerned to keep these laws. Josephus tells us of an incident from the days of Pontius Pilate which demonstrates the level of popular piety:[15]

Pilate ... introduced into Jerusalem by night and under cover the effigies of Caesar which are called standards. This proceeding, when day broke, aroused immense excitement among the Jews; those on the spot were in consternation, considering their laws to have been trampled under foot, as those laws permit no image to be erected in the city; while the indignation of the townspeople stirred the country-folk, who flocked together in crowds. Hastening after Pilate to Caesarea, the Jews implored him to remove the standards from Jerusalem and to uphold the laws of their ancestors. When Pilate refused, they fell prostrate around his house and for five whole days and nights remained motionless in that position.

On the ensuing day Pilate took his seat on his tribunal in the great stadium and summoning the multitude, with the apparent intention of answering them, gave the arranged signal to his armed soldiers to surround the Jews. Finding themselves in a ring of troops . . . the Jews were struck dumb at this unexpected sight. Pilate, after threatening to cut them down, if they refused to admit Caesar's images, signalled to the soldiers to draw their swords. Thereupon the Jews . . . flung themselves in a body on the ground, extended their necks, and exclaimed that they were ready rather to die than to transgress the law. Overcome with astonishment at such intense religious zeal, Pilate gave orders for the immediate removal of the standards from Jerusalem.

Despite Pilate's surprise over their reaction to what, for him, must have been standard military procedure, the Jews described here were not unrepresentative but epitomized ordinary people devoted to what they believed was God's Law. As such, they could not stand idly by while Roman soldiers marched into Jerusalem with images of the divine Caesar on their standards. The very presence of such images violated the commandment against idolatry in Exodus 20:4 and Deuteronomy 5:8.

Of course, many other laws required interpretation, if they were to be obeyed in a concrete manner. The priests in theory had the ultimate say in such matters and this certainly made sense when it came to running the Temple. Different groups of priests could disagree, however, as we saw in the last chapter with regard to the Qumran community. If 4QMMT is any guide, the sect's leadership believed the priests in charge of the Jerusalem Temple were in error over numerous points of the Law. And when it came to the practicalities of everyday life, the priests in Jerusalem could not monitor people's private behaviour any more than they could judge whether individual Jews were loving God with all their heart and might, as stipulated in Deuteronomy 6:5. Inevitably, therefore, the observance of whole portions of Jewish law was down to the disposition of ordinary Jews.

The resultant internalization of the Torah by Jews outside the priesthood may account for the rise of a group like the Pharisees. As explained earlier, they consisted largely of lay persons who became adept at interpreting the Law independently of the Temple authorities. Going beyond the basic requirement, they even adapted for themselves priestly purity rules which were not, strictly speaking, applicable to lay people. Moreover, Josephus hints that, when the Pharisees developed their own traditions about how real priests should perform their sacred duties, they clashed with the Sadducean Temple establishment.[16]

The question of how the Torah was to be interpreted could clearly provoke serious disagreement, although it seems that the majority of Jews were prepared to tolerate a degree of divergence. Unusually, the Qumran community 'separated' (4QMMT[d]) from the rest of Judaism as a protest over various contentious legal issues. Although most other Jews took a more conciliatory line, the extreme case of Qumran does serve to illustrate how resolute Second Temple Jews were in keeping God's commands. This central emphasis explains why so much literature from the period occupies itself with the subject of the Law in one way or another.

As observed at the outset of this section, it would be wrong to conclude that Jews experienced the detailed regulations contained in the Torah as trivial or oppressive. Neither was a legal preoccupation inimical to loving God and one's neighbour, or to a sense of dependency on divine grace. Once again, the first-hand evidence of the sectarian DSS, in the form of the hymn in 1QS 11:11–15, illustrates this point well:

As for me,
   if I stumble, the mercies of God
   shall be my eternal salvation.
If I stagger because of the sin of flesh,
   my justification shall be
   by the righteousness of God which endures for ever.
When my distress is unleashed
   He will deliver my soul from the pit
   and will direct my steps to the way.
He will draw me near by His grace,
   and by His mercy will He bring my justification.
He will judge me in the righteousness of His truth
   and in the greatness of His goodness
   He will pardon all my sins.
Through His righteousness He will cleanse me
   of the uncleanness of man
   and of the sins of the children of men,
that I might confess to God His righteousness,
   and His majesty to the Most High.

As this passage shows, the strict legalism of the Qumran community was by no means incompatible with a humble devotion to a God of love and grace.

II *The Place of Apocalyptic*

Alongside a pervasive and obligatory concern with the Law, Second Temple Jewish literature also reflects widespread speculation on a range of theological issues. Unlike obedience to the Torah, such matters were not considered binding. In other words, while adherence to the laws of the Pentateuch – however they were interpreted – was compulsory for everyone, matters of belief were not. Such doctrinal openness meant that, apart from elementary notions about God, Israel, the Temple, and the Law, Jews were free to believe more or less what they wished on all kinds of issues.

Such theological licence was made possible by the assumption that it was membership of the Jewish community, not correct belief, which brought redeemed status. Even the Qumran sect, although it judged only those of its own number to be true Jews, thought along these lines. For them and others, a person's place within the community of the faithful was maintained by obedience to the Torah, coupled with the conviction that God would forgive the shortcomings of those who were loyal to him.

The minimal dogmatic content of Second Temple Judaism was the corollary of its predominantly legal orientation. This accounts for the vast array of theological opinions current in Second Temple times. Indeed, a variety of doctrines evolved around the foundational notions of God, Israel, the land, the Temple and the Torah. Some of these ideas became fairly widespread in the course of the last two centuries BCE and the first century CE. It is likely, for example, that most Jews acknowledged the existence of angels and demons by the first century CE, partially in response to a growing sense of God's transcendence and a concomitant need for angelic intermediaries. As for life after death, the injustices manifest in this world required some kind of reversal in the hereafter in the eyes of many. According to Josephus, the main dissenting voice here was that of the Sadducees.[17] But, even with a popular notion like the afterlife, diversity prevailed. We saw this earlier when noting that, while Philo envisaged an immortal soul freed from the constraints of the body, Jews in Palestine tended to think in terms of a physical resurrection.

More exotic types of doctrinal speculation were the preserve of particular individuals or groups. In certain quarters, for instance, there was considerable interest in the figure of Enoch, mysteriously 'taken' by God without dying according to Genesis 5:24. The work known as 1 Enoch, a collection of five books which once existed separately, is presented as a revelation about a range of topics to its namesake. The fact that numerous copies were recovered from Cave 4 at Qumran is evidence that the secrets it purports to disclose were taken seriously by the community. Four of the books come from well before the sect was formed and try to encourage the reader in two ways. First, through Enoch's guided tour of the cosmos and its mysteries, as recounted in 1 Enoch 17–36, assurances are given that the wicked will eventually perish and the righteous be vindicated, despite appearances to the contrary. Second, the reader is reassured that, notwithstanding the turmoil of the times, history is unfolding in line with what is written on God's heavenly tablets (1 Enoch 93:2). Indeed, numerous points of detail show the author believed he lived near the end of time. As for the source of the world's ills, elaborating on the enigmatic passage of Genesis 6:1–4, 1 Enoch 6–11 maintains that they stem, not so much from the fall of Adam and Eve, but from a primordial act of fornication between angelic beings and human females.[18] Given that 1 Enoch probably circulated widely, this tradition would have been known among Jews outside Qumran too.

In contrast, the belief in the special status of the Teacher of Righteousness was a distinguishing mark of the group behind the sectarian DSS. This conviction was doubtless passionately held and members would have been glad to explain it to newcomers. Even so, this major doctrinal feature of the Qumran community seems to have taken a back seat in comparison to more urgent matters of the Law. Certainly, it was the correct application of purity rules which 4QMMT sought to impart to its addressees, rather than the Teacher's status, although their precise formulation may have derived from the Teacher or his associates.

The variety of theological opinions also forms the background against which we should understand Jewish hopes for the future in the Second Temple period. Scholars tend to employ the term 'eschatology', derived from the Greek adjective *eschatos* (meaning 'last' or 'final'), when referring to such hopes. As in other areas, so too a spectrum of views was tolerated. This meant that, apart from a general expectation that something good was in store for God's people, no one set of eschatological beliefs was universally current in the last two centuries BCE or the first century CE.[19]

Such hope could manifest itself in various ways. For example, the second-century BCE text Ecclesiasticus, in hoping for an improved version of the current state of affairs, looks primarily to the accession of an ideal High Priest. In contrast, the author of Daniel, writing in the middle of Antiochus IV's persecution of Judaism between 167 and 164 BCE, places his hope in imminent divine intervention. The supernatural and dramatic elements that feature in this sort of eschatology are often described as 'apocalyptic', because they tend to appear in the literary genre known as the 'apocalypse'. An apocalypse, a name which comes from the Greek word *apocalypsis* ('revelation'), is a type of writing which purports to be a direct revelation from God or an angel, like parts of Daniel and 1 Enoch.[20] It should be made clear, however, that a few apocalypses, such as Jubilees, have little that is apocalyptic. Conversely, some writings which are not set in the genre of the apocalypse contain considerable apocalyptic material, as in the case of 1QM from Qumran.

The arrival of a particular eschatological figure is sometimes expected to implement an improvement in the lot of God's people. Even here, though, much variety is in evidence. In 1 Maccabees, it is the whole line of Maccabee brothers and, by implication, their Hasmonean successors, who have fulfilled this role; because divine blessing has already been inaugurated, there is no future expectation. In the Psalms of Solomon, written soon after Pompey's capture of Jerusalem in 63 BCE, the author looks forward to a time when God will raise up a new king descended from the line of David to purify the Jewish nation and rid Jerusalem of the Gentiles. The figure concerned can be described as a 'Messiah', as long as it is remembered that the term simply means 'anointed one' and connoted no clearly defined notion. As we saw in relation to Qumran, almost any servant of God raised up for a special task could be described as 'anointed', including priestly and prophetic figures, as well as a descendant of David.[21] Only later did 'the Messiah' come to designate a fixed identity, as both Judaism and Christianity developed after the destruction of the Temple. Indeed, in some Jewish texts written before 70 CE, no anointed figure appears at all, the relevant functions being attributed directly to God himself. Still further removed from such notions is the book of Wisdom. This work, penned in Egypt at the turn of the era, contains hardly anything that could be described as eschatological, let alone apocalyptic. In good Platonic fashion, all the writer looks forward to is the release of the individual soul from the body at the hour of death.

THE TORAH TAKES OVER

The contrast between the binding status of the Law and the open-ended nature of doctrinal speculation we have just described was also a marked feature of Judaism after Second Temple times. However, the defeat of the First Revolt against Rome in 70 CE provoked a crisis within the Jewish community of a sort that had not been experienced since the Babylonians destroyed Jerusalem and took the people of Judah into exile in 587 BCE. More precisely, what had been two major focuses of identity – the Temple and the priesthood – were no longer able to function. Without these institutions, many of the legal prescriptions in the Pentateuch were unworkable. Sacrifice could not be offered, for instance, nor could certain purificatory rites be performed by the priests. In the face of these calamitous losses, Judaism had to reorient itself in order to survive.

The form such reorientation took may seem surprising at first. Essentially, the vacuum created by the demise of the Temple and the priesthood was filled by a devotion to the Torah which was even more wholehearted than that which had obtained before 70 CE. This meant that lay Jews, in particular, were able to continue observing the Torah in those areas which required neither a visit to the Temple nor the aid of the priesthood. In this limited way, obedience to the Law was able to retain its place at the heart of Jewish life, while matters theological remained secondary. Nevertheless, over a period of time, Judaism underwent a process of transformation at a deeper level. Even though it takes us beyond the world of the DSS, it is worth looking at what happened.

First of all, let us consider the changes brought about by the fall of Jerusalem in 70 CE. From this point on, we hear no more of the Sadducees, presumably because the destruction of the city and its Temple spelled the end of their power, wealth and priestly status. The community at Qumran, as we saw in Chapter 3, was put to flight in 68 CE; we do not know what happened to related Essene groups living elsewhere, of whom there is no mention whatsoever in Rabbinic literature, not even in the Mishnah of *circa* 200 CE. As for the Zealots, their humiliating defeat at the hands of the Romans ruled them out as contributors to the renewal of Judaism necessary in the aftermath of the Revolt.

With the demise of the Sadducees, Essenes and Zealots, as well as the general chaos that must have engulfed the lives of most ordinary Jews, it was left to a small group of rabbis to rescue the situation. They reshaped Jewish religion over a period of one hundred and fifty years, though their precise historical origins are unclear. As for the term 'rabbi', it is worth explaining that the word means 'teacher' in Rabbinic literature and became the standard designation for a religious leader, as the principal spiritual figures of Second Temple times, the priests, disappeared. Derived from the Hebrew adjective for 'great', the term could also mean simply 'sir', especially before 70 CE. It is likely, therefore, that the few occurrences of the word from the first century CE mean 'sir' or 'master' rather than 'rabbi' as a kind of title.[22]

As noted earlier, documents from 200 CE and later describe the rabbis of the Mishnah and Talmud in idealized terms. Thus, their founding father, someone called Yohanan ben Zakkai who was smuggled out of Jerusalem in a coffin while the city was besieged by Roman troops, is said to have headed a team of Torah experts who were heirs to the Pharisees.[23] Some elements in this story are clearly anachronistic or even legendary. Nevertheless, a core of early Rabbinic teachers established themselves in Yavneh, also known as Jamnia, to the north-west of Jerusalem, moving to the Galilean town of Usha during the second century CE.[24] As for the Pharisaic connection, it may contain a grain of truth. Yohanan ben Zakkai and his colleagues no doubt took as their starting point for the renewal of Judaism the elements of common Judaism outlined earlier. But, with the Temple and priesthood defunct, they had to concentrate, like the Pharisees before them, on laws which applied to the everyday life of lay people. Unlike the Pharisees, who had been able to benefit from the Temple when necessary, they had to find a way of making such day-to-day matters flourish as the mainstay of Judaism.

One of the ways they did this was through the synagogue. Although Second Temple Jews met for public reading of the Torah in prayer-houses or synagogues, it was only with the demise of the Temple that the institution came into its own. Bereft of the priesthood and sacrifice, Jewish communities throughout the world slowly made it an indispensable focal point of worship and learning. Understandably, as long as the Temple had stood, too much emphasis on the synagogue would have been inappropriate. After 70 CE, however, the partial borrowing of the language and imagery of the Temple in the liturgy and furniture of the synagogue helped the rabbis rescue Judaism and in time consolidate the community.[25]

More importantly, the rabbis after 70 CE also set about redefining the essence and scope of the Torah. The end result was embodied in the Mishnah, a compilation from *circa* 200 CE made up mostly of detailed legal debate.[26] The underlying notion of what the Torah is finds expression in one of the Mishnah's few theologically oriented portions, Avot (meaning 'Fathers' or 'Ancestors'). An abridged version of Avot 1:1–18 reads as follows:[27]

> 1. Moses received the Law from Sinai and committed it to Joshua, and Joshua to the elders, and the elders to the Prophets; and the Prophets committed it to the men of the Great Synagogue. They said three things: Be deliberate in judgement, raise up many disciples, and make a fence around the Law.
>
> 2. Simeon the Just was of the remnants of the Great Synagogue. He used to say: By three things is the world sustained: by the Law, by the [Temple-]service, and by deeds of loving-kindness.
>
> 3. Antigonus of Soko received [the Law] from Simeon the Just . . . 4. Jose b. Joezer of Zeredah and Jose b. Johanan of Jerusalem received [the Law] from them . . . 6. Joshua b. Perahyah and Nittai the Arbelite received [the Law] from them . . . 8. Judah b. Tabbai and Simeon b. Shetah received [the Law] from them

> ... 10. Shemaiah and Abtalion received [the Law]
> from them ... 12. Hillel and Shammai received [the
> Law] from them. Hillel said: Be of the disciples of
> Aaron, loving peace and pursuing peace, loving man-
> kind and bringing them nigh to the Law ...
>   18. Rabban Simeon b. Gamaliel said: By three
> things is the world sustained: by truth, by judgement,
> and by peace, as it is written, *Execute the judgement of*
> *truth and peace*.[28]

This passage starts off straightforwardly by recalling that, after
Moses received the Law from God, it was entrusted to success-
ive generations in the biblical period. However, from the 'men
of the Great Synagogue', the writer moves on to post-biblical
teachers, culminating at the start of the next chapter with Rabbi
Judah, the compiler of the Mishnah itself in around 200 CE.
While ethical and theological statements are associated with
the names appearing in Avot 1, the pronouncements attributed
to them in the rest of the Mishnah are overwhelmingly
legal.[29]

  The implications of the above are more far-reaching than
they might seem at first sight, especially when combined with
the evidence of other Rabbinic texts. Essentially, alongside the
Pentateuch or Written Law, God was thought to have revealed
to Moses a concomitant Oral Torah. Memorized and passed
on through the centuries, it was eventually written down in
the form of the Mishnah and, subsequently, the Talmud (*circa*
550 CE). The Oral Torah, in addition to laws purportedly
uttered by Moses himself, contained legal rulings made by
rabbis after 70 CE, which thereby were given a kind of Mosaic
authority by association. The resultant notion of the Dual
Torah, made up of both Written and Oral parts, constitutes
the most distinctive feature of Judaism as it developed in the
Rabbinic period. Not only did the Torah represent an absolute

revelation from God, but it was also able to incorporate the new legal decisions of the rabbis as they adapted the Law to the shifting circumstances of their own day.[30]

In common with Second Temple times, doctrinal matters were less of a pressing concern for the Rabbinic authorities. Apart from the most basic theological foundations of Judaism, which now included a belief in the bodily resurrection of the dead, Jews remained free to speculate as they wished.[31] For instance, some believed that Abraham, the founding father of Judaism, had kept the whole Law of God – even though it had not yet been revealed to Moses on Mount Sinai. Others pondered the status of the Gentiles in the divine scheme of things. However, little attempt was made to harmonize contradictory viewpoints on such matters, which, as a result, can often be found side by side in a given passage of the Talmud. While there seems to have been a universal expectation that God would one day restore the fortunes of his people, the same sort of open-endedness applied to eschatology. Although a standard hope for the advent of an anointed Davidic figure took shape in the Rabbinic period, the precise characteristics and activities of the Messiah were open to debate.[32]

Moreover, there was little that could be described as apocalyptic among the various aspects of future expectation popular after 70 CE. Many Second Temple Jews, in contrast, had been prone to think in apocalyptic terms, as the proliferation of apocalypses and apocalyptic themes demonstrates. With the defeat of the First Revolt, in which such notions had played a significant part, the rabbis of Yavneh seem to have rejected apocalyptic ideas. Although many ordinary Jews found such a change of heart more difficult, the defeat of a Second Revolt against Rome in 135 BCE finally convinced them of the dangers of the apocalyptic imagination.[33] In fact, it was probably this widespread realization that brought the majority of the Jewish population under the sway of the Judaism being formulated by the rabbis. Without ceasing to believe that God would one day restore his people, it now seemed best to leave the matter in his hands alone. What counted in the meantime was a whole-hearted devotion to the Torah as interpreted by the Rabbinic authorities.

Indeed, with the wide acceptance of the Mishnah (*circa* 200 CE), followed several centuries later by the Babylonian Talmud (*circa* 550 CE), Jewish life took on a homogeneity never seen before. Not only was everyone agreed that keeping the Law was the mainstay of Judaism, but now, with the rise to prominence of the rabbis and their interpretation of the Torah, everyone also agreed on how to obey it in practice. It is only from the third century CE, therefore, that we can speak of a normative Judaism.

THE DEAD SEA SCROLLS AND MODERN JUDAISM

We have seen that it was largely through the notion of the Dual Torah that the rabbis managed to salvage the situation that prevailed after the defeat of the First Revolt against Rome. By the time of the Talmud, the Dual Torah had eclipsed the need for a Temple or priesthood, because Judaism's most sacred rite was now the study of the Written and the Oral Law. Biblical heroes like Moses or David, accordingly, are portrayed in Rabbinic literature as Torah scholars devoted to keeping the commandments. Even God is presented on occasion as the student of the Torah *par excellence*, resembling something of a rabbi himself.

This religious system served the Jewish community well for over a millennium, so that, despite sporadic persecution, Jewish spirituality was able to flourish under Roman, Christian and Islamic rule. In the Middle Ages, moreover, Jewish philosophy and mysticism retained their essential Jewishness through the ongoing role played by the Torah.[34] From around 1800, however, the situation changed dramatically. Jews began to adjust in markedly different ways to life in the modern world. To complete this chapter's overall picture of Judaism, therefore, it is worth elucidating a little on this return to diversity. We shall then be able to close by considering briefly what impact the DSS might have on Judaism today.

Rather as in Second Temple times, modern Jews have responded divergently to the complex circumstances of the nineteenth and twentieth centuries. Among several factors which have elicited different responses, the fruits of historical study have been particularly important. We saw back in Chapter 2, for example, that scholars in the late 1800s began to question the Mosaic origin of the Pentateuch. In reaction to this and other issues, the Jewish community split into a number of denominations from the nineteenth century onwards. They still exist today and can be listed across a traditional–liberal axis: Hasidic (or ultra-Orthodox), Orthodox, Conservative, Reform (or Liberal), and Reconstructionist. Here, the most traditional are Hasidic Jews, whose outlook continues to be framed in terms of the Dual Torah; at the opposite extreme, Reconstructionist Jews prefer to see Judaism as an evolving human civilization, in which God and the Law are mythical elements. These two ends of the spectrum account for only a relatively small proportion of modern Jewry. In between, the Orthodox, Conservative and Reform camps encompass most Jews and each attempts to formulate an effective compromise with life in the modern world.[35]

Yet even among these three groupings considerable differences remain. At the top of the list comes the status of the Torah. Whilst Orthodox Jews continue to believe in its divine origin, Reform Judaism qualifies such belief by acknowledging the results of academic study. For the former, therefore, the laws of the Pentateuch and their elaboration in the Talmud remain obligatory commands from God, while the results of academic study tend to be held at arm's length. Reform Jews, however, modify the Law's revelatory status by accepting that historical and cultural circumstances shaped the traditions of Judaism over the ages as much as the divine will. Conservative Judaism takes up a midway position.

The two divergent standpoints of Orthodoxy and Reform give rise to opposing attitudes towards a range of practical issues. Day-to-day obedience to the Torah is the most obvious one. Orthodoxy maintains, for example, that the whole gamut of ancient dietary rules should be followed because their authority derives ultimately from God. Reform Jews, on the other hand, leave such matters to individual conscience, encouraging only those who find such rules meaningful in the modern world to follow them. On a more topical note, a similar split is evident over the role of women. Since the Talmud assumes that men alone are obliged to obey the full range of God's Law, with only negative commands in the main being applicable to women, it clearly makes no sense for modern Orthodox Jews to ordain female rabbis. Within Reform Judaism, however, this can be done without difficulty, for a more selective and creative approach to the traditions of the past is encouraged.[36]

From a neutral stance, it would obviously be wrong to suggest that the DSS directly support one manifestation of modern Judaism rather than another, whether the Orthodox, Conservative or Reform position. Neither do they easily connect to contentious issues, like the role of women, for most of the questions facing contemporary Jews would not have occurred to those living in Second Temple times. But it would be equally wrong to say that the DSS have nothing to contribute at a general level. Two observations stand out for comment in this regard.

The first has to do with historicity, for the DSS have a

two-fold lesson to teach us in this connection. On the one hand, the biblical DSS have made it difficult to uphold the traditional priority accorded to the MT, as we have seen, let alone the Mosaic authorship of the Pentateuch. Not only have they confirmed the general conclusions of earlier biblical scholars that most books, including the Law, were penned between 550 and 300 BCE, but they have also shown that many probably existed in multiple editions right from the start.[37] Simultaneously, the Pharisees can no longer be thought of as the guardians of mainstream Judaism in Second Temple times in a line going backwards to the Oral Law, also supposedly revealed to Moses, and forwards to its eventual codification in the Mishnah and Talmud under the leaders of Rabbinic Judaism.[38] On the contrary, the sectarian DSS have helped us reconstruct a picture of Judaism in the last two centuries BCE and the first century CE which is quite different: the Pharisees were one among several small religious parties with distinctive traditions of their own over and above the primary elements of common Judaism.

Clearly, therefore, inasmuch as the contemporary debate between Orthodox and Reform Judaism centres on such historical questions, the DSS form part of a wide body of evidence which favours a Reform position. Whatever positive value ancient Jewish traditions developed after 70 CE – like the status of the MT or the role of the Pharisees – may have, this much must be conceded. Indeed, having long accepted that the Pentateuch took shape soon after 550 BCE following a long period of growth, Reform Jews will not be disturbed to discover now that it also existed in divergent editions and that the portrait of the Pharisees found in Rabbinic literature is anachronistic. Yet there is more at stake than the mere acceptance or rejection of the historicity of events. This explains why modern Orthodox Judaism tends to keep at arm's length the full force of such conclusions.

Here, we must turn to our second observation which concerns the very nature of Judaism itself. The Orthodox position encourages the belief that at the heart of Jewish practice is a core of legislation revealed by God in a literal sense. As such, the laws of the Pentateuch and their elaboration in the Talmud are absolutes which, notwithstanding the degree of flexibility allowed when it comes to their precise application, cannot be annulled. This approach furnishes Orthodoxy with a consistency and certainty which many people find attractive or feel is a necessary part of any religion worth its salt. But it also means that its ability to change and adapt Jewish practice and belief has strict limitations. For example, there is little scope for dealing with the possibility that the cultural background of the writers of the Bible and the Talmud may have led them to frame their legislation in a manner which was inherently sexist. Thus, despite the dissatisfaction of increasing numbers of ordinary Orthodox women about what may be perceived as their secondary status, the official position remains more or less unchanged.[39]

From the Reform perspective, in contrast, such absolutes were shattered in the nineteenth century, when scholars began to conclude that the Mosaic authorship of the Pentateuch could no longer be sustained. The whole notion of a fixed revelatory corpus had to be tempered with the realization that Jewish traditions had in reality evolved considerably over the centuries – in biblical times, as well as in the Second Temple and Rabbinic periods and beyond. With no fixed point of revelation to appeal to, the only place where Jewish traditions could really have originated was always within the community itself. Furthermore, the members of each new generation, whether fully aware of it or not, have always reshaped earlier traditions to a degree that has only become apparent with modern academic study of the Bible and Judaism. Although accepting such scholarly conclusions inevitably has a relativizing effect on the way the traditions of the past are perceived, it also endows Reform Judaism with a capacity to adapt to life in the modern world by unashamedly remoulding ancient traditions, overtly rejecting others, and creating new ones of its own. Hence, for example, the Reform synagogue eventually felt able to ordain its first female rabbi in 1972. While this approach does not remove the need for God, the notion of Judaism as a revealed religion in a literal sense has to be dispensed with. Instead, God is deemed to be with the community in the ongoing dynamic process of reformulating its identity, as well as its practices and beliefs, from one generation to another.

In light of what we learned in earlier chapters, it would seem that the evidence of the DSS enhances this sense of the fluidity and dynamism of Jewish traditions, already recognized by the Reform movement. To that degree, especially when coupled with other relevant material from biblical, Second Temple and Rabbinic times, they also would seem to support a broadly Reform approach to Jewish tradition and its application to life in the modern world.

CHAPTER 5

Christianity Reconsidered

A CENTURY OF NEW TESTAMENT STUDY

Historical and literary investigation into the New Testament by scholars has been going on for over a century. One of the fruits of such work is the daunting body of academic literature that now exists on all aspects of every New Testament book. Nonetheless, many important lessons about the nature of Jesus' ministry and early Christianity have been learned, although, as in every other field, experts continue to disagree on innumerable points of detail.[1]

Lack of space rules out even the briefest survey of New Testament scholarship, nor can we analyse in detail particular biblical passages. However, several points can be distilled which will help us understand in the next two sections the similarities and differences between the Dead Sea Scrolls, on the one hand, and Jesus and early Christianity, on the other. We shall then be in a position, especially in view of the light shed in the last chapter on Second Temple Judaism at large, to ask what caused Jews and Christians to part company by the end of the first century CE. Having done so, the possible impact of the DSS on modern Christianity will be considered.

The first general point to be gleaned from over one hundred years of study concerns the original composition dates of the books of the New Testament. Most of them, even those which may have drawn on older sources, reached their final edition after 70 CE. All experts in the field would accept this conclusion on the basis of details in the text which are normally passed over unnoticed by most readers.[2] As with the Old Testament, it has been necessary to revise the traditional dates of authorship accepted by religious authorities for centuries. An example from Luke's Gospel will serve to illustrate what is involved. The words attributed to Jesus in Luke 19:41–44, rather than being a prediction of the future, seem to reflect a time when the defeat of the First Revolt of the Jews against Rome had already happened. As such, the passage must stem from after 70 CE, for we know that Christians subsequently interpreted the destruction of the Temple as a sign of divine disfavour on the majority of Jews who had not become Christians. Even if Luke's Gospel preserves the real words of Jesus elsewhere, therefore, in its present form it was composed as a whole after 70 CE.[3] Little store should be put by the tradition that the author was Luke the physician who accompanied the Apostle Paul on one of his missionary journeys during the 50s CE.[4]

A similar conclusion is likely with regard to the composition date of Mark, and inescapable when it comes to Matthew, John, the book of Acts and many letters in the New Testament. Included among the latter, several epistles traditionally believed to be the handiwork of Paul were almost certainly written after his death: Colossians, 2 Thessalonians, 1–2 Timothy, Titus and Hebrews. The main factor pointing in this direction is the theological disparity between them and other letters which are also attributed to Paul: Romans, 1–2 Corinthians, Galatians, Ephesians, Philippians, 1 Thessalonians, and Philemon. Most scholars are agreed that the best way of explaining the doctrinal incongruity between these two groups of letters is to suppose that only the latter eight were penned by Paul himself during the 50s CE. Consequently, they make up the earliest evidence for Christianity contained in the New Testament. As for the other letters, we saw in Chapter 2 that the pseudonymous association of a work with a hero from the past was not uncommon among Jews and Christians in the last few centuries BCE or the first century CE.

Our second general point comes as a corollary of what has just been described: the New Testament is not of one mind.[5] Certain motifs, it is true, are common or even universal, the most obvious case being the centrality of Jesus. But even here diversity is evident, for the precise role of Jesus is not everywhere the same. In the early chapters of Acts, for example, he is portrayed as a messianic prophet, who was rejected by the people, vindicated through resurrection, and is now ready to return in glory as God's special servant. In Paul's letter to the Romans, however, greater significance is given to Jesus' death as a kind of atoning sacrifice. Such differences in early Christian belief occurred as ideas developed independently among a variety of communities in different locations. Naturally, Christian believers over the centuries have tended to play down the divergences in favour of the real similarities that exist between New Testament books. Historians, on the other hand, find it more fruitful to highlight variation. A further illustration may help. Some New Testament passages, like Romans 13:11–12 or 1 Corinthians 16:22, make it clear that the first Christians expected Jesus to return soon in apocalyptic splendour as part of the divine plan of salvation. Towards the end of the first century, though, Christians had to face the fact that such expectations had not materialized. The resultant adjustment in outlook is reflected in a context like 2 Peter 3:3–10. It is worth citing part of the passage:

[3]First of all you must understand this, that in the last days scoffers will come, scoffing and indulging their

own lusts [4]and saying, 'Where is the promise of his [Jesus'] coming? For ever since our ancestors died, all things continue as they were from the beginning of creation!'

. . . [8]But do not ignore this one fact, beloved, that with the Lord one day is like a thousand years, and a thousand years are like one day.

While the author believes in theory that Jesus could come back at any moment, the fervour of earlier writings has gone. In 2 Peter, therefore, we see Christians coming to terms with the idea that they might have to wait some time before Jesus returns.[6]

Our third and final point has to do with what can be known of the historical Jesus himself and those early Christians who lived in the 30s, 40s or 50s CE. Given the late and varied nature of most New Testament books, what is said about Jesus and the Apostles in the Gospels and Acts cannot necessarily be taken at face value. Nevertheless, complete scepticism is not in order. By carefully reading between the lines, it is possible to recover at least an outline of what the historical Jesus was like. Likewise, several sermons incorporated into Acts 2–4 probably contain genuine recollections of the early Christian message. So, to Jesus and earliest Christianity and the relationship of both to the DSS we may now turn.

WAS JESUS AN ESSENE?

Over the past hundred years or so there have been many attempts to trace the contours of the life and work of Jesus of Nazareth. The main source for such reconstructions has, of course, been the New Testament, even though the oldest copies we possess are in the form of witnesses from the third and fourth centuries CE.[7] The suggestion that scraps of several New Testament books were found in Cave 7 at Qumran has been rejected by virtually all experts in the field, including the proposal that Mark 6:52–53 has survived in the form of 7Q5.[8] The latter is a small fragment containing twenty Greek letters, half of which are unclear. Without new evidence to substantiate the claim, therefore, the equation of 7Q5 with a portion of Mark is no more than a remote theoretical possibility which need not detain us.[9]

It is not practicable to present a survey of the numerous reconstructions of the historical Jesus that have been proffered over the years. With hindsight, however, it is interesting to note that a rather naive optimism at the turn of the century had given way to an equally unrealistic scepticism by the mid-twentieth century.[10] Fortunately, in the last twenty years or so a cautious optimism has come to dominate academic study of the life and work of Jesus. Among several important scholars in the English-speaking world are Geza Vermes of Oxford University, already mentioned in connection with the DSS, and E. P. Sanders of Duke University.[11] These and other experts would agree that some basic facts about the historical Jesus are recoverable, although a biography in the modern sense is well beyond reach. For the sake of readers who are unfamiliar with this kind of New Testament study, it is worth outlining the picture of Jesus' ministry that can be accepted with a high degree of probability.

Most scholars accept that Jesus was born just before Herod the Great died in 4 BCE (see Matthew 2:1–2) and was executed while Pontius Pilate was Prefect of Judaea between 26 and 36 CE (note, for example, Mark 15:1). If the statement in Luke 3:23 that Jesus was 'about thirty years old' is to be believed, then he probably embarked on his public ministry in the late 20s CE after encountering John the Baptist's message of repentance.[12] With John's execution, Jesus became an itinerant preacher and healer in his own right. As a Jew, he doubtless accepted the main elements of common Judaism, including the requirement to obey God's commands as set out in the Torah. Several stories in the Gospels show this was indeed the case, like the account in Mark 1:42–44 of Jesus' exhortation to a healed leper:

> [42]Immediately the leprosy left him, and he was made clean. [43]After sternly warning him he sent him away at once, [44]saying to him, 'See that you say nothing to anyone; but go, show yourself to the priest, and offer for your cleansing what Moses commanded, as a testimony to them.'

Whatever is to be made of the secrecy imposed on the former leper, Jesus sent him to be ritually cleansed by a priest because this was required by the Torah after leprosy. However, the story's wider context also implies that Jesus' main concern was to instil in people a renewed sense of faith in God, particularly among those who were disadvantaged by disease, poverty or sin. Such devotion was especially necessary in view of the imminent arrival of the Kingdom of God. This phrase is not defined, but Jesus seems to have employed it to designate the impending advent of God's kingly rule, bringing salvation for his people and the defeat of evil. There is no evidence that Jesus engaged in direct political or military action, for the power of God about to be unleashed on the world deemed it unnecessary. What the people experienced as exorcisms, healings and other miracles through his ministry, though, were signs that the Kingdom of God was near. It was this eschatological fervour that constituted the driving force behind Jesus' role as the proclaimer of 'good news', rather than any particular belief about his own identity.

After working in Galilee, Jesus spent the last phase of his

ministry, which probably lasted about one year in total, in Judaea and Jerusalem. At the time of one of the busiest Jewish festivals, the Passover, Jesus was arrested in Jerusalem. At a superficial level, the Gospel passion narratives (Matthew 26–27, Mark 14–15, Luke 22–23) explain his subsequent execution as a result of doctrinal disputes with the Jewish leaders of the time. This presentation, however, most likely reflects religious rivalry between Jews and Christians after 70 CE.[13] The real cause of Jesus' death was probably more mundane, for, as both Josephus and Acts testify, several independently-minded spiritual leaders were dealt with harshly during the 40s and 50s CE for the sake of political expediency. As in these cases, it is probable that Jesus was killed by the authorities, not because of his religious message *per se*, but to avoid the risk of social upheaval consequent upon the popular success of his ministry.[14]

Lack of space precludes adding further details to this bare reconstruction which, in any case, would require us to choose between the dissenting opinions of scholars. Nevertheless, even the above outline makes it highly unlikely that Jesus was an Essene, given what we have already learned about the DSS. Such a negative conclusion does not mean there were no similarities between Jesus' message and that of the Essenes. The most noticeable link is a common note of repentance against the background of eschatological urgency. This finds expression in 1QS's exhortation to keep the sect's interpretation of the Law in anticipation of imminent divine intervention, as well as in Jesus' call to believe the 'good news' of the impending advent of God's kingdom. With this kind of general parallel, however, the similarities end. Thus, while it is fair to assume that Jesus shared the common Jewish attachment to the Torah, we have no evidence that he cared for the sort of detailed preoccupation with its application that inspired the Essenes. The fact that Jesus preached openly to the Jewish crowds, moreover, is contrary to the Essene commitment to secrecy evident in both the sectarian DSS and in Josephus' accounts. In addition, Jesus lived and worked towards the end of the period during which the Essenes existed; as we also saw in relation to the Zealots, this chronological factor militates against identifying Jesus simply as an Essene.

Jesus might have had an association with the Essenes before he embarked on his ministry, ceasing to be one of their number only when he began to preach and heal. But the truth is that we know next to nothing about Jesus before he started his public career. The birth narratives in Matthew 1:18–2:23 and Luke 1:5–2:40, as well as the report about Jesus as a boy in Luke 2:41–52, are clearly legendary.[15] His previous religious affiliations, therefore, are a matter which must be left entirely open.

A better case for some form of Essene link can be made in relation to Jesus' forerunner, John the Baptist. The limited information we have about this man comes mainly from Mark 1:4–8, Matthew 3:1–12 and Luke 3:1–20. All three accounts agree that John lived in the desert 'preaching a baptism of repentance for the forgiveness of sins' (Mark 1:4) and that his work prepared the way for Jesus. Like Jesus and the Essenes, John appears to have had a heightened eschatological sense of the urgency of his message. More significantly, he lived in the desert and engaged in baptismal or purificatory rites in a manner reminiscent of the practices enjoined in the sectarian DSS. Once more, however, caution is in order. Although it is possible that he had previously been a member of the Qumran sect, by the time he was carrying out the work ascribed to him in the Gospels, John could no longer have been an Essene. As with Jesus, the public nature of his proclamation is in stark contrast to their preference for secrecy. And, when it comes to the common connection with the wilderness, we noted back in Chapter 1 that the desert of Judaea functioned as a sanctuary for a variety of religious and political groups throughout Second Temple times and beyond.

To sum up, the testimony of the DSS, when set alongside an informed reading of the Gospels, forces us to conclude that Jesus was not an Essene. Neither did John the Baptist belong to the Essene movement – at least, not while engaged in his public preaching mission. At the same time, the luxury afforded by the evidence of the DSS has shown up significant parallels between the message of the documents from the caves, on the one hand, and the ministry of Jesus and his forerunner, on the other. Taken together, these overlaps demonstrate just how Jewish John and Jesus must have been. There is certainly nothing to suggest that either of them intended to found a new religion. On the contrary, both are best understood when placed fully within the world of Second Temple Judaism.

THE DEAD SEA SCROLLS AND EARLY CHRISTIANITY

A similar evaluation of the evidence holds for the relationship between the DSS and early Christianity immediately after Jesus. Despite some real parallels, it is clear that the early Christians were not Essenes. Apart from any other factor, like John the Baptist and Jesus, the Christian movement arose at the end of the period during which the group behind the sectarian DSS flourished. Furthermore, the early Christians engaged in open preaching among all Jews and, eventually, Gentiles in a way that separates them from the Essenes. The main distinguishing feature of early Christianity, however, was its emphasis on Jesus of Nazareth. In contrast, there are no explicit references to Jesus in the sectarian DSS or in the classical accounts of the Essenes by Philo, Josephus or Pliny.[16] Neither, as far as we can tell, does he feature cryptically in the documents from Qumran. As we saw in Chapter 3, the names that do appear in the latter are best set against the background of the second and first centuries BCE.[17] It can safely be stated, therefore, that, despite recent claims to the contrary, no New Testament character is mentioned in any of the DSS. There are no grounds for directly linking the two communities historically by way of either common persons or events.

Nevertheless, a comparison of the sectarian DSS and the writings of the New Testament does show up a number of interesting parallels. Of all the religious groupings current in Second Temple Judaism, the early Christians may well have had most in common with the Essenes. It is worth spelling out two overlaps of a general nature and three which are more specific.

The first has already been touched on, for, as will be clear by now, both the sect at Qumran and the early Christians had a strong eschatological orientation. Each group believed in its own way that God was on the verge of intervening dramatically in human affairs. This theme constitutes a thread through the Gospels, Acts and genuine letters of Paul, on the one hand, as well as through sectarian DSS like 4QMMT, CD, and 1QM, on the other. Furthermore, both communities went through a period of crisis when the end of the world failed to materialize as expected. Just as 2 Peter 3:3–10 sought to reassure Christians that history was still on course, so 1QpHab 7:5–14 had dealt with a similar problem nearly two hundred years earlier, as the following excerpt, 1QpHab 7:5–8, evinces:

> *For there shall be yet another vision concerning the appointed time. It shall tell of the end and shall not lie* (ii, 3a).
>
> Interpreted, this means that the final age shall be prolonged, and shall exceed all that the Prophets have said; for the mysteries of God are astounding.

However, the first-century BCE Qumran writer, unlike his first-century CE counterpart, went on to exhort his readers to persevere in their obedience to the sect's interpretation of the Law.

Alongside a common eschatological preoccupation, several items of vocabulary mark a second general overlap. It has often been remarked that the Hebrew term in 1QS usually translated as 'the Congregation' (Hebrew, *ha-rabbim*, meaning literally 'the many') is similar to Paul's reference to 'the majority' (Greek, *ton pleionon*) in 2 Corinthians 2:6. Again, the designation 'overseer' or 'bishop' (Greek, *episkopos*) in some New Testament books (for example, Philippians 1:1 and 1 Timothy 3:1–7) appears to be equivalent to the 'Guardian' or 'Overseer' (Hebrew, *mevaqqer*) of the Qumran texts (see 1QS 6:12). These and other terminological links have shown that many early Christian turns of phrase must have originally been Aramaic or Hebrew expressions subsequently translated into Greek as the Church grew beyond the confines of Palestine.[18] They also demonstrate that, like John the Baptist and Jesus before them, the early Jerusalem Christians were thoroughly embedded within the world of Second Temple Judaism.

Besides such general similarities, some closer parallels also exist. Bible interpretation, in particular, is a noticeable feature of both the early Christians and the Essenes. Just as we categorized a whole class of Qumran literature on the basis of its utilization of scripture, so many New Testament writings expound the contents of the Old Testament in terms of the first century CE rather than the time of the original biblical authors. Scattered through the Gospels, for instance, scriptural references are adduced to support Jesus' proclamation that the Kingdom of God is near. Other New Testament works cite biblical verses to lend weight to the early Christian message. In Acts 2:14–17, Peter explains to the puzzled crowds standing by that Joel 2:28–32 has been fulfilled in the glossolalia of the early Christians:

[14]But Peter . . . raised his voice and addressed them, 'Men of Judea and all who live in Jerusalem, let this be known to you, and listen to what I say. [15]Indeed, these are not drunk, as you suppose, for it is only nine o'clock in the morning. [16]No, this is what was spoken through the prophet Joel:

[17]"In the last days it will be, God declares,
   that I will pour out my spirit upon all flesh,
   and your sons and your daughters shall prophesy,
   and your young men shall see visions,
   and your old men shall dream dreams."'

This Christian parallel to the Qumran treatment of the Old Testament shows that similar assumptions underlay usage of the Bible in both communities.

Here and there, in fact, the same scriptural passage is employed in both the sectarian DSS and the New Testament. Habakkuk 2:4, for example, is cited and interpreted in 1QpHab 7:17–8:1–3 and Galatians 3:11–12, as the following arrangement indicates:

1QpHab 7:17–8:3	NRSV
[*But the righteous shall live by his faith*] (ii, 4b).	[11]Now it is evident that no one is justified before God by the law; for 'The one who is righteous will live by faith'. [12]But the law does not rest on faith; on the contrary, 'Whoever does the works of the law will live by them.'
Interpreted, this concerns all those who observe the Law in the House of Judah, whom God will deliver from the House of Judgement because of their suffering and because of their faith in the Teacher of Righteousness.	

However, close scrutiny of these two passages shows that the same biblical text was handled differently by the authors in question. Despite similar assumptions about the Bible at a general level, the distinctive messages of the two communities encouraged divergent interpretations of concrete biblical passages. Thus, Habakkuk 2:4 is used by Paul to bolster his contention that trust in God is distinct from obedience to the Torah. The Qumran author, on the other hand, employs the same verse to emphasize that true faith and adherence to the sect's interpretation of the Law are one.

Another link between the early Christians and those at Qumran concerns doctrinal speculation about individuals. For instance, both communities chose the figure of Melchizedek, 'priest of God Most High' according to Genesis 14:18, as an object for theological reflection. The New Testament letter to the Hebrews appeals to him typologically as a basis for viewing Jesus as a heavenly High Priest, even though, like Melchizedek, he was not descended from the priestly line of Aaron. In 11QMelch, the same biblical figure is equated with the Archangel Michael and predicted to defeat Satan at the end of time. For this author, both Melchizedek and other angels are called *elohim*, the regular Hebrew word for 'God'. Because certain obscure Old Testament passages, like Exodus 21:6 and Psalm 8:6, use the term to mean 'judge' or 'angel', however, Melchizedek's designation as *elohim* does not denote his literal divinity but his eschatological role as a supernatural judge on behalf of God.

More generally, the figure envisaged in 11QMelch is the biblical Melchizedek himself, albeit equated with the Archangel Michael of the book of Daniel. Hebrews draws on the figure of Melchizedek as a mere type in relation to the status of Jesus. Despite striking similarities, therefore, the treatment of Melchizedek by the Essenes and early Christians was different. This is hardly surprising, for we learned in the last chapter that numerous biblical heroes could be subjected to doctrinal speculation in a variety of ways.[19]

Unique to both the Qumran sect and the early Christians was a focus on their respective founders, the Teacher of Righteousness and Jesus. Attachment to these special individuals was what marked out the two religious movements as distinct from each other, as well as from the other Jewish parties that flourished in the late Second Temple period. Here too, though, what seems to be an exact parallel at first sight fails to stand up to close scrutiny. For those at Qumran, the Teacher had a vital but restricted role both as founder and as an inspired interpreter of the Law, while at least two further messianic figures were expected to arrive in the future.[20] For the early Christians, in contrast, Jesus subsumed within his person all such roles. We can turn again to Hebrews to illustrate this point, for the writer portrays Jesus as both Davidic Messiah and as a high-priestly figure.[21]

A final important link between the Qumran community and early Christianity has to do with a common aspect of organization attested nowhere else in the late Second Temple period. According to Acts 2–5, the early Christians in Jerusalem practised a kind of communal ownership. Acts 4:32 implies that each drew from a central fund according to his or her needs:

> Now the whole group of those who believed were of one heart and soul, and no one claimed private ownership of any possessions, but everything they owned was held in common.

This description is remarkably similar to what is commended in 1QS. Furthermore, as with the Essenes, it seems that some Christians retained private property, for Paul assumes as much in 1 Corinthians 16:2. This more relaxed arrangement parallels the approach found in CD 14:12–13, which stipulates that members contribute only a proportion of their income to a common fund.

What are we to make of these substantial overlaps between early Christianity and the religious group behind the sectarian DSS, especially the close organizational parallels in matters of property? We have already seen that it is not possible to equate the two communities. It is possible, however, that some individuals joining the early Christian movement had an acquaintance with the Essenes and their practices; some may even have been former Essenes. This could explain the similarities in organization just described. A few scholars, indeed, have argued that, from the days of Herod the Great, there was an Essene Quarter in the south-western part of Jerusalem which, by the first century CE, was in close proximity to the earliest Christian community.[22] Unfortunately, the evidence only amounts to Josephus' reference to an 'Essene Gate' in Jerusalem and his statement that Herod looked favourably on the Essenes at the start of his reign.[23] While some Essenes probably did live in Jerusalem, as in other towns in Palestine, the existence of a special Essene Quarter next to the first Christian meeting-place requires much more proof. Equally plausible in the meantime is the suggestion that Essene organizational practice was common knowledge and that, for want of a better model, early Christians adopted and adapted it to their own needs.

Yet, when it comes to the shared eschatological zeal, the parallel usage of the Bible, and speculation on particular figures, a broader explanation is in order. In short, the two communities developed along similar lines in certain respects because they were both zealous Jewish sects which sprang from the shared world of late Second Temple Judaism. If this is an accurate portrayal, then the prime impact of the sectarian DSS on our understanding of early Christianity is to show that the early Christians were essentially another Second Temple Jewish party which came into being during the first century

CE. Although some in the first half of this century had an inkling that this might be the case, it is only as familiarity with the DSS has increased in recent decades that such a conclusion has become obvious to most working in the field. All New Testament experts, in fact, would now accept this reconstruction, although a number of older books still in circulation assume that Jesus or the first Christians had broken with Judaism in a fundamental way. In reality, the main distinguishing feature of the first Christians was simply that, alongside a basic adherence to common Judaism, they assigned a unique place in the divine schema to Jesus of Nazareth. They also tried to persuade others Jews of his special anointed role and, not surprisingly, the term Messiah was applied to him. Given Jesus' unique standing among early Christians, that word soon became a title, 'the Messiah', and was translated into Greek as 'the Christ' which, in turn, became a kind of surname in the designation 'Jesus Christ'.

FROM JEWISH PROPHET TO GENTILE GOD[24]

The above description applies to the early Christian movement as it took shape in and around Jerusalem during the mid-first century CE. From a careful reading of Acts 1–5, it can be deduced that, as well as believing in Jesus, its members continued to keep the Sabbath, circumcise their sons, attend worship at the Temple, and adhere to the dietary and purity laws of the Torah. Indeed, as the sectarian DSS have demonstrated in relation to the Essenes, a distinctive devotion to a particular figure did not imply any fundamental break with Judaism.

So, how and when did Christianity become a religious tradition separate from Judaism? Here, we must turn to the Apostle Paul, for he introduced one critical innovation which slowly transformed early Christianity from a Jewish sub-group into a fully-fledged Gentile religion. Paul argued that non-Jews should be allowed to enter the Christian community without converting to Judaism. In so doing, he was doubtless driven by his conversion, recounted in Acts 9:1–22 and Galatians 1:13–17, and by an awareness that the success of his Gentile mission would be limited if adult male converts had to undergo the unpleasant rite of circumcision. According to Acts 15 and Galatians 2, Paul's plea for the admittance of Gentiles as Gentiles, a development not envisaged by Jesus or the first Christians, was opposed by the leaders of the Jerusalem Church.[25]

Nevertheless, a compromise was reached. The Jerusalem Apostles would concentrate their efforts on bringing other Jews into the Christian fold, while Paul would work among Gentiles without insisting they convert to Judaism. In Galatians 2:7–9, he describes this arrangement in his own words:

> [7]On the contrary, when they saw that I had been entrusted with the gospel for the uncircumcised, just as Peter has been entrusted with the gospel for the circumcised [8](for he who worked through Peter making him an apostle to the circumcised also worked through me in sending me to the Gentiles), [9]and when James and Cephas and John, who were acknowledged pillars, recognized the grace that had been given to me, they gave to Barnabas and me the right hand of fellowship, agreeing that we should go to the Gentiles and they to the circumcised.

As it transpired, Paul's missionary efforts had considerable success. He was no doubt helped by the existence of sizeable numbers of 'God-fearers' – Gentiles who, attracted by Judaism, attached themselves to Diaspora synagogues without actually converting.[26] Yet, faced with mixed Jewish–Gentile congregations, Paul had to strike a careful balance when it came to his main religious focus. He did this by concentrating on Jesus, the only common element uniting all who had responded to his message.

Paul's doctrinal reflections enabled him to build up his congregations without alienating either the Jewish or Gentile side. In Romans 5–7, for example, he expounds the benefits that fall to the Christian who has died and risen with Jesus by virtue of being 'in Christ' through baptism. Such theological elaboration was comparable to that found among other Jewish movements. We saw earlier how 1 Enoch enlarges on the figure of Enoch, while the Qumran sect gave a special place to the Teacher of Righteousness. Thus, Paul included in Philippians 2:6–11 an early Christian hymn which speaks of Jesus Christ:

> who, though he was in the form of God,
> > did not regard equality with God
> > as something to be exploited,
> but emptied himself,
> > taking the form of a slave,
> > being born in human likeness.
> And being found in human form,
> > he humbled himself
> > and became obedient to the point of death
> > – even death on a cross.
> Therefore God also highly exalted him
> > and gave him the name
> > that is above every name,
> so that at the name of Jesus
> > every knee should bend,
> > in heaven and on earth and
> > under the earth,
> and every tongue should confess
> > that Jesus Christ is Lord,
> > to the glory of God the Father.

Jesus is on the verge of divinity here and in a few similar passages. As with Melchizedek's designation as *elohim* in 11QMelch, however, the language used falls short of full deification, for, as long as Jewish monotheism prevailed in the background, this was impossible. With that proviso, it was permissible to employ hyperbolic language to describe figures like Enoch, Melchizedek, the Teacher of Righteousness or Jesus, deemed by their respective communities to have a special function in the divine plan.

However, Paul's admission of Gentiles as Gentiles into the communities he founded meant that increasing numbers of Christians had no real attachment to common Judaism. According to Galatians 3:27–28, mystical union with Jesus rendered other distinctions – including that between Jew and Gentile – of no consequence. In other words, the Jewishness of Jewish Christians was no longer important. Not surprisingly, as the numbers of Gentiles grew, Jewish Christians who kept the Law had less and less in common with Gentile Christians. This state of affairs meant that, during the second half of the first century CE, there was little encouragement for Jewish Christians outside Palestine to remain committed to common Judaism. As for Gentile Christians, without the requirement to convert to Judaism, the Torah was little more than a source providing typological lessons from the past. Indeed, most Christian writers of the late first century CE were occupied with further doctrinal speculation about Jesus and his work, as can be seen in letters like 1–2 Timothy, where Christian identity is framed in an increasingly non-Jewish way.

This process had reached a climax by the time the Gospel of John was written. Stemming from around 100 CE, it refers frequently to 'the Jews' as though they formed an entity completely separate from the author and his community. The implication is that most Christians were not Jews by this stage and, vice versa, nearly all Jews stood outside the Christian movement. Although the seeds of this split were sown by Paul's policy towards the admission of Gentiles, it was probably the defeat of the First Revolt against Rome which precipitated the final rupture between Jews and Christians.

On the one hand, the destruction of the Temple in 70 CE was interpreted by Christians as divine retribution on the majority of Jews for not accepting the Christian message. On the other, the predicament of Jews after 70 CE required a renewed commitment to the main elements of Jewish practice for the sake of Judaism's survival. Hence, Jewish Christians were faced with an impossible dilemma. Some presumably left the Church in favour of full involvement in the synagogue; others stayed within Christianity and, in so doing, ceased to identify themselves as Jewish. Such circumstances probably lie behind the Rabbinic denouncement of 'heretics' in Jewish writings of the late first and second century CE. The same situation informs the attack on the Pharisees in Matthew 24, where Jesus and the Pharisees represent the Christians and the Rabbinic authorities of the writer's own day; it also explains the negative references to 'the Jews' in John's Gospel.

These developments had a momentous effect on Christian doctrine. John's Gospel, indeed, explicitly identifies Jesus as divine. John 1:1–4, equating Jesus with the eternal Word of God, is the best known example:

> In the beginning was the Word, and the Word was with God, and the Word was God. [2]He was in the beginning with God. [3]All things came into being through him, and without him not one thing came into being. What has come into being [4]in him was life, and the life was the light of all people.

In this way of thinking, hyperbolic words and motifs which had not previously implied Jesus' deity, because set within the monotheism of common Judaism, were now taken to indicate divinity. The Gospel of John and 1 John are the only New Testament books which have taken this bold step and elaborated their doctrinal position accordingly. The Christians responsible were probably unaware of just how much their theological formulations violated Jewish notions of God. For Jews, such doctrines compromised traditional Jewish monotheism and transformed Christianity into an independent Gentile religion.

Of course, it is not for us, as historians, arbitrarily to approve either the Jewish or Christian position just set out. More neutral is the supposition that each side was responding to the circumstances of the time as seemed appropriate. In any case, a growing number of scholars are reaching the same broad conclusion when it comes to understanding the parting of the ways between Jews and Christians.[27] And, as has hopefully come across already, the DSS have provided much of the relevant framework by highlighting the priority given to the Law in Second Temple Judaism over and against secondary matters of theological speculation. It was primarily the abandonment of the former, therefore, not doctrinal elaboration about Jesus in itself, which divided the Christian movement from Judaism towards the end of the first century.

THE DEAD SEA SCROLLS AND THE CHURCH TODAY

In subsequent centuries, Christian belief and practice developed even further. In the area of doctrine, the Nicene Creed (325 CE), the Apostles' Creed (*circa* 390 CE), and the Chalcedonian Definition (451 CE) provided a core of beliefs to which all Christians were supposed to adhere.[28] Thus, doctrines like the Incarnation and Trinity became essential elements of Christian orthodoxy. Naturally, it was thought that such beliefs, if not spelled out explicitly in the New Testament, were at least implied in its pages. This assumption remained the norm when the Christian world split into East (Orthodox) and West (Catholic) in the eleventh century and with the schismatic effects of the Protestant Reformation during the fifteenth and sixteenth centuries.

With the advent of modern academic study of the New Testament, however, this presumption began to be questioned. At the same time, new knowledge was coming from other quarters. As outlined in Chapter 2, analysis of the Old Testament overturned many traditional notions of authorship and date, while challenges of a different sort emanated from the work of Darwin and Freud. As a result, from the nineteenth century many Christian Churches spawned a spectrum of theological wings which set up camp within existing denominations. The resultant fault lines can be characterized in traditional– liberal terms and continue to exist in varying degrees inside the Roman Catholic and Anglican Churches, for example, as well as within and between Protestant groups. Consequently, Christians now take up a variety of positions on a number of contentious issues, some of which – like the ordination of women or the place of homosexual people within the community – hit the headlines of the press from time to time.

The DSS do not address such specific issues, as hardly needs to be stated in view of what has been learned in previous chapters. Nor do they impinge directly on the validity of this or that type of modern Christianity. Nevertheless, such a valuable and ancient collection of Jewish literature from a group which lived at the time of the first Christians may, in combination with other evidence, have some bearing on contemporary Christian identity. Two observations in this regard are in order.

First, although the DSS do not link up directly with early Christian personalities or events, we have seen that their contribution to our understanding of the wider world of Second Temple Judaism indirectly casts light upon early Christianity. Scholarly analysis of the Qumran community, with its combination of legalism and belief in the Teacher of Righteousness, helped us conclude that there is no reason to think the first Christians intended to break with Judaism. Where New Testament writings seem to assume otherwise, they almost certainly reflect a situation prevailing after the success of Paul's missionary activity, when Christians began to lose sight of their historical origins and even started to misapprehend the nature of Jewish religion. Much of the Jewish community's suffering within Christendom over the centuries can be explained as a result of this tragic misunderstanding.[29] More positively, the DSS contribute to a range of factors which has encouraged modern Christians over the past forty years or so to reconsider their Jewish origins, as well as relations with contemporary Judaism.[30]

Second, the DSS have highlighted the diversity of Second Temple Judaism. The early Christians, indeed, were part of the varied nature of Jewish religion in the first century CE. Not only were several distinct religious parties current in late Second Temple times, but each group itself appears to have gone through various stages of development. Certainly, we have seen this in relation to the DSS and the New Testament, both of which reflect changes in the practices and beliefs of their respective communities. Yet this internal diversity creates problems for anyone seeking theological or moral guidance from the pages of the New Testament – as it would, theoretically speaking, for anyone wishing to utilize the sectarian DSS as scripture in the same sort of way. Because the ancient writers were not of one mind themselves, modern Christians seeking to distil lessons from the Gospels, say, or from the Pauline corpus may find themselves in something of a dilemma.[31] As implied at the end of our last chapter, a similar dilemma faces

Jews who accept the results of academic study of the sacred texts of Judaism.

The DSS, however, may add a potentially constructive twist to this second observation. It concerns the imagination of the Essenes, particularly evident in the sect's interpretation of the biblical text. 1QpHab 11:9–15, for instance, illustrates a masterful control of biblical sources:

> *You have filled yourself with ignominy more than with glory. Drink also, and stagger! The cup of the Lord's right hand shall come round to you and shame shall come on your glory* (ii, 16).
>
> Interpreted, this concerns the Priest whose ignominy was greater than his glory. For he did not circumcise the foreskin of his heart, and he walked in the ways of drunkenness that he might quench his thirst. But the cup of the wrath of God shall confuse him . . .

Each biblical phrase has a counterpart in the commentary. Thus, *You have filled yourself . . . with glory* is applied to 'the Priest whose ignominy was greater than his glory', while *Drink also, and stagger!* denotes his drunkenness as a sign of impiety and *The cup of the Lord's right hand* prefigures the Wicked Priest's punishment. But what about 'For he did not circumcise the foreskin of his heart'? In the biblical citation, 1QpHab reflects the LXX's *Drink and stagger* as a way of emphasizing the subject's wickedness. However, the MT here reads 'Drink and show your uncircumcision', uncircumcision being a parallel metaphor for impiety. As it happens, 'stagger' and 'show your uncircumcision' look similar in Hebrew and this explains the discrepancy between the MT and LXX. It is more interesting, though, that the author of 1QpHab was unencumbered by the existence of such conflicting readings. He employed both creatively for his own purposes.

This sort of creativity informs a lot more of the sectarian

DSS than might appear at first sight, for neither the Torah nor books like Isaiah or Habakkuk came ready-interpreted from God. Even if the Teacher of Righteousness and other leaders of the sect were not fully aware of the extent of their own contribution, there is surely a lesson here for modern Jews and Christians. In other words, maybe the array of religious traditions that have flourished in the past, often all the more bewildering and contradictory for being subjected to academic analysis, presents an opportunity for the imagination. Indeed, it is arguable that, like the writer of 1QpHab, Jews and Christians throughout the ages have always creatively selected and reshaped existing traditions in order to make sense of the circumstances of their own day.

CHAPTER 6

Controversy
and Conspiracy

TWO RECENT COUNTER-THEORIES

We have seen so far that a broad consensus has emerged over the past forty or fifty years. The best way of explaining the ruins at Qumran and the manuscripts found in the surrounding caves is to connect both with the Essenes mentioned by Philo, Josephus and Pliny. Such a hypothesis enables us to account for most of the relevant evidence in a consistent manner, including the DSS released for the first time in late 1991. It also allows us to paint a picture of the religious sect itself, as well as the state of the biblical text available at Qumran and, presumably, elsewhere in Second Temple times. Furthermore, the DSS help us enter more fully than ever before into the world of both Second Temple Judaism at large and that of nascent Christianity.

However, whilst the majority of experts would assent to these general conclusions, the breadth of the resultant consensus should be emphasized. Within it are many variations and disagreements on points of detail. We saw earlier, for example, that an increasing number of scholars view the Qumran community as a splinter group which seceded from a wider Essene movement. Yet others have tried to counteract this trend by reworking the earlier direct identification of the Qumran sect with the Essenes.[1]

Several proposals of late have dispensed with any Essene connection or else doubted the link between the ruins at Khirbet Qumran and the documents recovered from the nearby caves. In this section, therefore, we shall review an attempt to revive a Sadducean hypothesis, as well as a radical proposal linking the DSS with the well-to-do of Jerusalem. In the following section, the merits of two alternative theories regarding the function of the Qumran site will be evaluated. The remainder of the chapter will then proceed to examine three sensational proposals that have received much media attention. Finally, we shall close with a consideration of the reasons for such ongoing fascination with documents which are some two thousand years old.

I   *Resurrecting the Sadducees*

One challenge to the Essene hypothesis has come from Lawrence Schiffman of New York University. For some time, he has been promoting the theory that the community at Qumran was a group with strong Sadducean links.[2] The evidence adduced by Schiffman centres on legal positions advanced in both the sectarian DSS and in the Mishnah.

The Mishnah is a lengthy work, made up of over sixty tractates, or chapters, and was compiled around 200 CE, although many of the traditions it contains are doubtless older. Essentially, it sets out to apply the laws of the Pentateuch to the shifting circumstances of everyday life and, as part of its programme, contains a tractate called Yadaim which deals with matters of ritual purity. One of its sections purports to recall some of the legal conflicts between the Pharisees and Sadducees of Second Temple times. Yadaim 4:7, in particular, is worth noting:[3]

> The Sadducees say, We cry out against you, O ye Pharisees, for ye declare clean an unbroken stream of liquid. The Pharisees say, We cry out against you, O ye Sadducees, for ye declare clean a channel of water that flows from a burial ground.

The language employed by the Mishnah here can seem rather inaccessible to the unpractised reader. But the basic point at issue concerns how ritual impurity is transmitted. In the first sentence, we are told that the Sadducees believed impurity could be transmitted from a pot into which water was being poured, back up the stream of liquid, into the other dish from which the liquid was being emptied. The Pharisees, apparently, disagreed. While the subject under discussion may not seem very interesting in itself, Schiffman's point is that the same legal stance attributed to the Sadducees in the Mishnah turns up in the important Qumran text known as 4QMMT:[4]

> [55]Also, concerning streams (of liquid), we say that they have no [56]purity, and that such streams do not separate the impure from the [57]pure. For the liquid of streams and that in the receptacle are alike, [58]being one liquid.

Schiffman is doubtless right to detect agreement between the Yadaim passage and this excerpt from 4QMMT.

On several counts, however, it does not necessarily follow that the group at Qumran was Sadducean. Apart from anything else, we saw earlier that other elements can be isolated which seem to show a link between the DSS, on the one hand, and the Pharisees or even the Zealots, on the other.[5] In general terms, this should come as no surprise, for there must have been some similarities between the different religious parties of the Second Temple period. Just as the various religious denominations of our own day overlap in certain respects, so too presumably did those in the last two centuries BCE and first century CE. Such occasional agreements are insufficient in themselves to identify the Qumran community as Sadducean.

Nevertheless, Schiffman has reaffirmed his commitment to a Sadducean link in a recent book.[6] In view of legal parallels of the kind exemplified above, he traces the Qumran community to a nucleus of Sadducean dissidents opposed to Jonathan Maccabee's accession to the High Priesthood in 152 BCE. Although they subsequently developed in distinctive ways of their own, that Sadducean link, Schiffman argues, should predominate in debates about the identity of the community and its relationship with other Jews.

Schiffman is unlikely to persuade most scholars of his position for three main reasons. First, several elements present in the sectarian DSS – including belief in angels and the resurrection of the dead – were rejected by the Sadducees according to Josephus. Those behind the Qumran documents were either not Sadducees at all, therefore, or had moved so far beyond a Sadducean position that an original connection tells us little of their subsequent identity. Second, Schiffman dismisses out of hand the cumulative evidence linking the DSS with the Essenes of the classical sources. As already observed in Chapter 3, most scholars have been swayed by the consistent nature of such overlaps which outweigh real but intermittent connections with the Sadducees, Pharisees or Zealots. Third, many will handle Schiffman's volume with caution in view of an allegation he makes at the outset. He accuses other scholars of misreading the DSS over the years by relating them almost exclusively to early Christianity instead of the history of Judaism. As even a brief scan of the works listed in earlier chapters of this book will demonstrate, however, this charge is simply not true.

II *Did the Dead Sea Scrolls Come from Jerusalem?*

Professor Norman Golb of Chicago University has posed another challenge to the Essene hypothesis.[7] In his view, no Essenes lived at Qumran at all, for, as we shall see in the next section, he has argued that the site was a fortress unconnected with the sect. Nor is the hotchpotch of texts from the nearby caves to be identified as an Essene library, according to Golb. Rather, the literature constitutes the random contents of Jerusalem libraries taken to the caves for safety in the late 60s CE as the Roman siege of the city commenced.

So, what arguments does Golb adduce in favour of his alternative hypothesis? First, he believes the DSS collection is too large and diverse to have been the property of a small religious party. Most of the documents, indeed, are not sectarian but consist of books from the Bible, Apocrypha, Pseudepigrapha and other works which were probably circulating widely. As for the so-called sectarian texts, they advocate a variety of contradictory views on a range of issues like marriage and, as such, cannot represent the single viewpoint required by the Essene hypothesis. And the presence of one supposedly sectarian composition, Shirot 'Olat ha-Shabbat, in both Cave 4 (4QShirShab) and at the Zealot stronghold of Masada shows that some of the documents were in fact employed by groups of different persuasions. In Golb's judgement, therefore, the DSS came from a number of wealthy individuals or groups who secreted their books in the caves as the Romans advanced on Jerusalem. If this is correct, he maintains, it is unnecessary to harmonize the contradictory elements in such a haphazard collection.

Second, Golb dismisses the evidence of Pliny the Elder, cited in Chapter 3, as irrelevant because Pliny set his description of the Essenes in the present tense. Since his work was published in 77 CE, by which time Qumran had been destroyed, Pliny's Essenes must surely have been resident somewhere else. A third objection raised by Golb concerns an apparent lack of accounts and other domestic documents which would have been essential if the DSS belonged to an independent religious sect which existed over a period of time.

Golb has expanded the main substance of his thesis in a recent book.[8] However, he appears not to have taken full account of the releases of fresh material in late 1991. He assumes, for instance, that the 'Jonathan' praised in 4QapPs & Jon must be the Hasmonean leader Alexander Jannaeus whose Hebrew name was indeed Jonathan. This text, he argues, constitutes another nail in the coffin of the Essene hypothesis, which takes it for granted that the Hasmonean line was the sect's worst enemy.[9] But in reaching this conclusion, Golb seems unaware that the 'Jonathan' concerned could just as easily be Jonathan Maccabee. Professor Geza Vermes of Oxford has suggested as much, pointing out that, according to 1QpHab 8:9–10, he was respected by the putative leaders of the community in the formative years of the sect.[10]

Similarly, even if some of the documents known as 4Q3442–359 actually came from Murabba'at or Nahal Hever, which, as we have seen, now seems to be the case, a few of them may still have been retrieved from Cave 4.[11] If that supposition proves to be correct, one of Golb's objections to viewing the DSS as the property of an independent religious community will be removed. But even if it does not, his other objections to an Essene hypothesis have failed to persuade scholars over the years, not least because Golb neglects to take account of alternative viewpoints with sufficient seriousness.

Thus, the fact that Pliny's description is in the present tense should not be allowed to outweigh the dramatic, if general, nature of his testimony. Since Pliny elsewhere freely admits to incorporating a large number of sources into his *Natural*

History, moreover, it would be wise to conclude simply that he drew on a pre-existing account of the Essenes which had been written before the Qumran settlement was abandoned in 68 CE.

Golb's most serious point concerns the diverse nature of the literary corpus found in the caves, which, in his view, precludes ascribing the whole collection to any one group of Second Temple Jews. Obviously, if he is correct, then the conclusions we reached earlier are erroneous. The evidence he puts forward, however, is, at the very least, capable of being interpreted otherwise. Several factors make Golb's theory a less likely explanation of the Dead Sea Scrolls phenomenon than what was proffered in Chapter 3.

First of all, the fact that much of the collection consisted of widespread biblical, apocryphal and pseudepigraphal works is only to be expected, for these books were the common scriptural heritage of all Second Temple Jews. Apart from anything else, the sect would have required copies of its own so that, through the interpretative skills of its leaders, it could persuade insiders and outsiders alike of the validity of its beliefs and practices. A second factor relates to the sectarian documents themselves. Aside from the most popular books (like Deuteronomy, Isaiah, Psalms, 1 Enoch, or Jubilees), most biblical books are extant in only one or two samples. In contrast, multiple copies of 1QS, CD, 4QMMT and other compositions have survived – documents which exhibit characteristics of an obviously partisan nature. Furthermore, despite real differences or even contradictions among the sectarian DSS, the thread of distinctive emphases which binds them together is more substantial than Golb allows.

Finally, the suggestion that, as the Roman siege began, Jerusalem's best and brightest slipped out of the city with hundreds of documents and carried them all the way to Qumran has struck most scholars as rather implausible. Preferable by far is the supposition that the contents of the eleven caves were linked to the site of Qumran, which for a considerable time was used by some kind of Essene community.

As if pre-empting the final point of the last section, Golb has allied his theory about the DSS with an alternative evaluation of the Qumran ruins.[12] The Qumran site, he maintains, did not belong to any religious community, but was, in fact, a fortress with no connections to the DSS whatsoever. To support this claim, Golb points to several features of the settlement which, initially at least, seem to back his case. Not only were the buildings surrounded by substantial walls, but a tower also stood at the heart of the site which was serviced by an extensive water system. The fact that the settlement was destroyed by military attack, moreover, acts as a further pointer to its own military use, argues Golb.

Actually, his theory is not entirely new. Back in the late 1940s, de Vaux thought that Khirbet Qumran had been a fortress unconnected with the manuscripts recovered from Cave 1. But he soon changed his mind after further excavations, and his revised conclusion still holds good. Apart from anything else, if Qumran was a fortress, it was an extremely bad one. Its walls, for instance, are not thick enough for effective defence, while the design of the water-supply would have laid it open to attack. In these circumstances, the tower would only have offered a temporary sanctuary to the inhabitants of the site. As for Golb's deduction from Qumran's destruction, we have not the slightest reason to think that Roman soldiers were in the habit of restricting their attacks to military installations. Due to objections such as these, in fact, no other eminent scholar has seen fit to follow Golb in his hypothesis.

Another theory about the nature of the Qumran ruins has been proposed recently by one of the archaeologists involved in preparing the final excavation reports never completed by de Vaux. Pauline Donceel-Voute, like Golb, has concluded that the settlement was not occupied by a religious community at all. Rather, she is of the view that Khirbet Qumran was a villa.[13] Central to her argument is the identity of the location known as Room 30.[14] The remains discovered there included debris from the collapsed first storey that had once stood over the ground floor, among them bits of brick and plaster. Their shape allowed De Vaux to piece them together to form what he identified as the table and benches of what must have been a kind of 'scriptorium' or writing-room. Donceel-Voute, however, has proposed that the reconstructed artefacts were more likely to have been dining furniture. Khirbet Qumran, on this hypothesis, was the villa of a wealthy person and the upper level of Room 30 was a dining-room. Accordingly, de Vaux's writing-table was actually a reclining sofa of the type common in Hellenistic and Roman times. Similarly, what were previously thought to be inkwells must have been some other sort of utensil employed in the dining-room.

Once more, though, the evidence is more convincing when interpreted differently. The main item of furniture from Room 30, as de Vaux reconstructed it, was 50 centimetres wide, 70 centimetres high, and several metres long. If it had been the sofa of a dining-room, as Donceel-Voute has proposed, it would have been unique in the ancient world, for reclining sofas were generally much wider than 50 centimetres. Indeed, it would have been difficult not to fall off such a narrow piece of furniture which, according to a recent study, would not have been strong enough to cope with such usage anyway.[15] In short, de Vaux's characterization of the Qumran site as a religious settlement and of Room 30 as a 'scriptorium' remains the best explanation of the evidence to date.

It should not be thought that every aspect of the theories presented by Schiffman, Golb or Donceel-Voute is simply untenable. On the contrary, these are able scholars, some of whose individual suggestions on particular facets of the evidence are plausible. However, the main argument against their hypotheses is the persuasiveness of a wide variety of other factors whose cumulative force is not treated sufficiently seriously. In light of the data we amassed earlier on, the best option still seems to be a version of the Essene hypothesis championed in Chapter 3, linking the DSS, Khirbet Qumran and the Essenes described by Pliny, Philo and Josephus.

THE DEAD SEA SCROLLS AND THE VATICAN

Beyond the renewed scholarly interest in the DSS exemplified in the theories described above, inspired in large measure by the fresh releases of late 1991, the scrolls have also attracted a lot of general media attention in the last few years. Numerous books aimed at a popular audience have claimed to shed new light of one sort or another on the nature of the DSS and, by implication, Judaism and early Christianity. Space will not allow an exhaustive account of all these proposals, but we can consider three of the most significant ones in this and the next two sections.

Back in 1991, two journalists, Michael Baigent and Richard Leigh, caused a sensation when they published a work provocatively entitled *The Dead Sea Scrolls Deception.*[16] In it, the authors set themselves three major tasks. Most straightforwardly, they provided a more-or-less accurate account of the DSS discovery and how the Essene hypothesis emerged as a scholarly consensus in the 1950s and 1960s. Because we have already reviewed the relevant data, this aspect of their work requires no further comment.

Secondly, however, the journalists went on to disclose that the Essene hypothesis was the result of a conspiracy to suppress DSS material which posed a threat to the Christian tradition.[17] To those with little or no prior knowledge of the subject area, their argument could appear convincing, for Baigent and Leigh draw on several factors which are true. Thus, the reader of their book is informed of the delay in publishing the documents from Cave 4 and the restrictions on access to the scrolls before late 1991. It is also explained that most members of the small editorial team were or became Roman Catholic and had an association with the college known as the Ecole Biblique et Archeologique de Jerusalem Française. As a Roman Catholic institution, it is further pointed out, the latter operated under the auspices of the Vatican in Rome.

On the basis of these observations, all of them sound enough in themselves, Baigent and Leigh founded their main accusation. The Vatican, they charge, directed the editorial team headed by de Vaux and was at pains to control the interpretation of the DSS in order to protect traditional Christianity. To that end, the main function of the Essene hypothesis was artificially to separate the DSS chronologically and theologically from early Christianity. Baigent and Leigh argue, moreover, that Cave 4 material was withheld over the years to prevent the damage to Christian belief which would have resulted if certain texts had entered the public domain.

Those who have followed the thread of this book so far may suspect that the real delusion in *The Dead Sea Scrolls Deception* is the conspiracy theory propagated by the authors themselves. But in view of the wide publicity their book received, it is worth spelling out why its contents cannot stand. Of the many individual criticisms that could be made, three broad observations are fatal to the hypothesis of the two journalists.

Most importantly, Baigent and Leigh do not fully appreciate that some elements in the Essene hypothesis derived from scholars who were outside the narrow clique headed by de Vaux. Geza Vermes, for example, was the first to argue seriously that the Wicked Priest of 1QpHab was probably Jonathan Maccabee. At the same time, Vermes was one of the most vociferous critics of the editorial team's scandalous publication record before the release of Cave 4 documents in the autumn of 1991.

Secondly, contrary to the impression given by Baigent and Leigh, the Ecole Biblique has a world-wide reputation when it comes to academic study of the Bible. Indeed, the institute's journal, *Revue Biblique*, remains at the cutting edge of modern Biblical Studies. It produces scholarly articles representing a range of opinions from a variety of scholars – whatever their personal religious convictions – on all the major aspects of Old Testament, Second Temple Jewish and early Christian history. When it comes to academic freedom and integrity, therefore, neither the Ecole Biblique nor the *Revue Biblique* can be characterized as under the thumb of the Vatican.

The Dead Sea Scrolls Deception's conspiracy theory is further undermined by a third observation: several proposals contrary to the Essene hypothesis have been put forward by Roman Catholic writers. We briefly observed earlier, for instance, that a Spanish Jesuit, Jose O'Callaghan, tried to make a case for identifying some Cave 7 fragments with portions of the New Testament. Similarly, Father Joseph Fitzmyer of the Catholic University of America, Washington D.C., has been among those who have criticized the original editorial team for failing to publish Qumran documents. These Catholic scholars can hardly be characterized as toeing a Vatican line. Whatever the real shortcomings of de Vaux and others, Baigent and Leigh's theory of a Vatican cover-up cannot be sustained.

The same negative judgement has to be passed on Baigent

and Leigh's third major theme, which concerns the true identity of the community behind the DSS. In the main, their views in this regard are derived from Robert Eisenman of California State University, Long Beach, whose name crops up frequently in the book. To his position, therefore, we may now turn.

THE DEAD SEA SCROLLS AND JAMES THE JUST

For over ten years, Eisenman has been trying to persuade other scholars that the Teacher of Righteousness was really James the brother of Jesus who, according to Josephus, was executed by the High Priest Ananus in 62 CE. This Ananus, in Eisenman's opinion, was the Wicked Priest of 1QpHab, while the Liar of CD was the Apostle Paul. Because the Gospels, in Eisenman's view, were composed in the second century CE, long after Paul had effected his transformation of Christianity, virtually nothing can be known of the historical Jesus, except that his execution was politically motivated. Cast by Eisenman as the ancient equivalent of a secret agent, Paul reinterpreted Jesus' death as a universal atoning sacrifice and thereby successfully remodelled early Christianity into a peaceable movement acceptable to the authorities.[18]

Christianity before Paul, in contrast, was legalistic, nationalistic and xenophobic, according to Eisenman. It emerged from a broad Zealot movement which can be traced back centuries and also incorporated the community at Qumran. Central to the argument he formulates is 1QpHab 11:3–8. This passage, interpreting Habakkuk 2:15, was cited earlier but is worth repeating:

> *Woe to him who causes his neighbours to drink; who pours out his venom to make them drunk that he may gaze on their feasts* (ii, 15).

> Interpreted, this concerns the Wicked Priest who pursued the Teacher of Righteousness to the house of his exile that he might confuse him with his venomous fury. And at the time appointed for rest, for the Day of Atonement, he appeared before them to confuse them, and to cause them to stumble on the Day of Fasting, their Sabbath of repose.

Back in Chapter 3, we saw that this excerpt probably speaks of the second-century BCE founder of the group behind the DSS and his opponent, Jonathan Maccabee. The 'house of his exile' in that case refers to Qumran or, possibly, some earlier outpost used before Qumran was settled.

Eisenman, however, wrongly translates 'house of exile' as 'place of concealment' and equates it with Jerusalem. Without any corroboration for such an identification, he then links 1QpHab 11:3–8 with Josephus' account of the execution of James the brother of Jesus – known in later Christian tradition as James the Just:[19]

> ... Ananus thought that he had a favourable opportunity because Festus was dead and Albinus was still on the way. And so he convened the judges of the Sanhedrin and brought before them a man named James, the brother of Jesus who was called the Christ, and certain others. He accused them of having transgressed the law and delivered them up to be stoned.

The incident described here is set in 62 CE, just after the rule of the Procurator Porcius Festus, but before the arrival of Clodius Albinus. The new High Priest, Ananus, decided to demonstrate his toughness by picking on James, the leader of the relatively small and, from Ananus' viewpoint, unimportant Jewish–Christian community in Jerusalem.[20] Eisenman asserts that it is this event which is reflected in 1QpHab 11:3–8.

Without supportive evidence, however, there is no basis for such an interpretation of the passage, let alone for taking it as the foundation for other elements in his imaginative theory.

Eisenman, along with Michael Wise of Chicago University, produced in 1992 the first widely available edition of some of the most important newly released Cave 4 documents.[21] Although the Hebrew or Aramaic texts and their English translation tend to be reasonably accurate, the accompanying comments reflect Eisenman's idiosyncratic interpretation of the DSS. One composition calls out for particular attention, 4QRule of War, fragment 5. In his introduction to this document, Eisenman holds that the work refers to the violent death of the Messiah. He translates the fragment as follows:[22]

> . . . Isaiah the Prophet, ['The thickets of the forest] will be fell[ed with an axe] (2) [and Lebanon shall f]all [by a mighty one.] A staff shall rise from the root of Jesse, [and a Planting from his roots will bear fruit.'] (3) . . . the branch of David. They will enter into Judgement with . . . (4) and they will put to death the Leader of the Community, the Bran[ch of David] (this might also be read, depending on the context, 'and the Leader of the Community, the Bran[ch of David] will put him to death') . . . (5) and with woundings, and the (high) priest will command . . . (6) [the sl]ai[n of the] Kitti[m] . . .

While bracketing an alternative, Eisenman maintains that this passage supports his own thesis that a broad Zealot movement, informing both the Qumran community and early Christianity, expected a messianic figure to undergo a political execution. Although there is no evidence to suggest that any Second Temple Jews thought in this way, Eisenman had already been prominent in earlier press reports in the first flurry of excitement after the release of new texts in autumn 1991.[23] He had maintained, in particular, that 4QRule of War showed that both the Qumran community and the early Christians shared a belief in the death of the Messiah.

However, for all that the ambiguous form of the relevant verb means Eisenman's translation is possible, the following rendering by Vermes makes better sense:

> [As it was said by] Isaiah the Prophet, *[The thickets of the forest] will be cut [down with an axe and Lebanon by a majestic one will f]all.* And there shall come forth a shoot from the stump of Jesse [. . .] the Branch of David and they will enter into judgement with [. . .] the Prince of the Congregation, the Br[anch of David] will kill him [. . . by strok]es and by wounds. And a Priest [of renown?] will command [. . . the s]lai[n] of the Kitti[m . . .]

Justification for this translation comes from the other fragments of 4QRule of War and from the context surrounding Isaiah 10:34 which is cited. These have the victory of God's anointed over the enemy in view, not his death. Indeed, this is the overwhelming picture that emerges from all Second Temple Jewish texts which anticipate the advent of a messianic figure modelled on King David. It is therefore entirely reasonable to suppose that the unique Christian emphasis on the Messiah's death was formulated, quite understandably, after Jesus' death had taken place.

More generally, Eisenman dismisses out of hand the cumulative effect of carbon dating, palaeography and archaeology.[24] While no one would deny that such techniques have their limitations, their overall impact is fatal to his argument, for we learned earlier that these methods point very strongly to the second and first centuries BCE as the likely background of the sectarian DSS. Certainly, 4QCalendar C lists several first-century BCE figures, while no first-century CE personage is explicitly mentioned anywhere.

Finally, one more fragment deserves comment. An Aramaic Apocalypse, dubbed 4QarApocal, contains some language which is remarkably close to that in Luke 1:32, 35. The Qumran document, damaged in places, reads as follows:

I. . . dwelt on him. He fell down before the throne . .
O [K]ing, you are angry for ever and your years . . .
your vision and all. For ever you . . . [the gre]at ones.
An oppression will come to the earth . . . a great massacre in the province . . . the king of Assyria [and E]gypt
. . . he will be great on earth . . . will make and all will
serve . . . he will be called (or: call himself) [gran]d . . .
and by his name he will be designated (or: designate
himself). II The son of God he will be proclaimed
(or: proclaim himself) and the son of the Most High
they will call him. Like the sparks of the vision, so
will be their kingdom. They will reign for years on
the earth and they will trample all. People will trample
people (cf. Dan. vii, 23) and one province another
province . . . until the people of God will arise and all
will rest from the sword. Their (the people of God's)
kingdom will be an eternal kingdom (cf. Dan. vii, 27)
and all their path will be in truth. They will jud[ge]
the earth in truth and all will make peace. The sword
will cease from the earth, and all the provinces will
pay homage to them. The Great God (cf. Dan. ii, 45)
is their helper. He will wage war for them. He will
give peoples into their hands and all of them (the
peoples) He will cast before them (the people of God).
Their dominion will be an eternal dominion (Dan. vii,
14) and all the boundaries of . . .

The verbal similarities with the Gospel of Luke are real enough, although they were in fact known to the scholarly world over twenty years ago.[25] However, it is not clear who the 'son of God' is. Not surprisingly, Eisenman has linked the passage to his theory of Christian origins, but more sober suggestions have also been made.

The figure could be understood positively as an angelic being (like Melchizedek) or as the future Messiah of David expected in some sectarian DSS. Since 2 Samuel 7:14 refers to King David (and his descendants) as God's son, this would not be unusual. Alternatively, the son of God in 4QarApocal could be understood negatively. In that case, he would be some idolatrous divine pretender, either from the past (like Antiochus IV) or anticipated in the future. Because the document draws on the language of Daniel, where this motif is prominent, the second is the more likely option.

AN HYPOTHESIS TOO FAR!

An even more sensational theory has come from the pen of Barbara Thiering of the University of Sydney, Australia, although she had previously written several useful articles on the Qumran world.[26] In 1992, however, she produced a book called *Jesus the Man: A New Interpretation from the Dead Sea Scrolls*.[27] To those with a basic familiarity with Second Temple Judaism and the DSS, it is not difficult to see that its contents belong to the realm of fantasy. But for others, the provocative title, combined with detailed appendices and lengthy footnotes, gives the work a semblance of hefty scholarship. In view of the publicity it received, therefore, we shall explain why Thiering's thesis is untenable after describing some of its main themes.

Essential to Thiering's rewriting of Qumran history, as to

Eisenman's, is her insistence that the sectarian DSS pertain chiefly to the last one hundred years of the Second Temple period. In other words, 1QpHab and related works have to do with people and events of the first century CE, not, as was argued in Chapter 3, the second and first centuries BCE. To justify this claim, Thiering re-dates the sectarian DSS, stating that palaeographical dates ascribed to individual documents by others should be given a wider berth of fifty years or so to account for several potentially misleading factors. She argues one-sidedly, for instance, that some first-century CE scribes may have deliberately written in an old-fashioned hand, while a false impression of antiquity could be given if a text were penned by a scribe still in training under an older master.

. Upon these shaky foundations, Thiering proceeds to discredit the main elements of the scholarly consensus. The reference to the Wicked Priest in 1QpHab 8:9–10 constitutes a good example. As we saw earlier, because he was 'called by the name of truth when he first arose' but fell from grace when he 'ruled over Israel', Jonathan Maccabee seems to have been intended here. Yet, for Thiering, 'Israel' in this passage means the Qumran sect, not the whole of the Jewish people, while 'truth' denotes its special teaching, rather than general uprightness. The crucifixion described in 4QpNah 1 is similarly relocated by Thiering in the first century CE as a depiction of Pontius Pilate's reaction to the protest over Roman standards bearing Caesar's image. Readers will remember that we cited the relevant passage from Josephus back in Chapter 4.[28] Because he records that Pilate quietly withdrew his troops without exacting punishment, however, it is the cruel action of Alexander Jannaeus in the first century BCE that must remain the most likely background against which we should view 4QpNah 1.

Thiering nevertheless continues to construct a first-century CE setting for the main sectarian DSS. Thus, the opponent of the Wicked Priest and hero of the Qumran community, the Teacher of Righteousness, is equated with none other than John the Baptist. This identification is based on the fact that the Hebrew word for 'teacher', *moreh*, could, grammatically speaking, also be taken as 'sprinkler' in the sense of baptizer. According to Thiering, John became the leader of the Essene movement which incorporated traditional and liberal wings in tension with each other. John himself belonged to the traditional side and believed the end of the world was near. Because he thereby threatened the religious and political status quo, Herod Antipas had him executed in 31 CE.

Before his death, however, the Essene movement experienced serious internal conflict. Tension between the Torah-centred traditionalists and the less rigorous universalist side is reflected in 1QpHab 11:5–8, where we learn that, as noted in Chapter 3, the Teacher of Righteousness was pursued by the Wicked Priest. In Thiering's opinion, this character was none other than Jesus of Nazareth. The tearing of the heavens in Mark 1:9–11, she argues, is a cryptic reference to the same dispute:

> In those days Jesus came from Nazareth of Galilee and was baptized by John in the Jordan. [10]And just as he was coming up out of the water, he saw the heavens torn apart and the Spirit descending like a dove on him. [11]And a voice came from heaven, 'You are my Son, the Beloved; with you I am well pleased.'

On the basis of this sort of decodifying interpretation of the Gospels, Thiering claims to be able to reconstruct the life of Jesus in remarkable detail. Accordingly, Gospel references to Galilee and Jerusalem actually denote the Judaean desert and Qumran. Moreover, married to Mary Magdalene (by whom he had two children), Jesus was an illegitimate descendent of King David, whom the sect expected to ascend the royal throne of Israel. He led the liberal faction within the Essene movement which was less Torah-oriented and less nationalistic, but more Gentile-friendly, than the wing represented by John the Baptist.

To cut a long story short, Jesus went too far even for some of his own supporters when, although a Davidic descendent himself, he dressed in the apparel of the High Priest – an incident which Thiering believes can be recovered from the transfiguration story in Mark 9:2–8. This and earlier misdemeanours, intolerable in the eyes of traditionalists, explain why Jesus is referred to as the Wicked Priest in 1QpHab. After a further disappointment, Judas Iscariot eventually betrayed Jesus as a potential insurgent to Pontius Pilate. Consequently, the Prefect of all Judaea rode out to Qumran for the trial of Jesus who was subsequently crucified just outside the settlement. As if that were not enough, on the basis of the reference in Mark 15:36 to the 'sour wine' offered him at his crucifixion, Thiering works out that Jesus was not killed by this ordeal. Rather, under the influence of snake poison, he was merely rendered unconscious and, after burial in Cave 7, was revived with herbs. Thereafter, he stayed at Qumran for a period, separated from Mary Magdalene, married a second wife (Lydia of Philippi in Acts 16:14), accompanied Paul on missionary work and ended up in Rome, where he is presumed to have died an old man.

To those who have worked their way through preceding chapters of this book, it should be clear already that Thiering's hypothesis is pure fantasy. Just in case any doubts remain, however, it is worth highlighting three reasons for such a negative judgement. First, while it is good to question current theories and re-evaluate existing evidence, Thiering's attempt to cast doubt on the work of others amounts to special pleading. She wrongly assumes, for example, that the inexact nature of the science of palaeography necessarily favours her younger dates for the sectarian DSS. In reality, allowing an extra fifty years' latitude in palaeographical dating could just as easily lead in the opposite direction. The Accelerator Mass Spectrometry tests published in 1992 and 1995 have shown, in any case, that the DSS collection centres on the first century BCE, with the first century CE at the tail-end of the relevant period.[29]

Secondly, persons mentioned by name in the sectarian documents clearly point in the same direction. 4QpNah 1:2–3, as observed several times before now, mentions an Antiochus and a Demetrius who are almost certainly Antiochus IV and Demetrius III of the second and first centuries BCE, respectively. Among the texts released for the first time in 1991, furthermore, we saw also that 4QCalendar C lists, among others, the first-century BCE figures of Salome Alexandra and Aemilius Scaurus. In contrast, no concrete historical figure from the first century CE is named in any sectarian DSS. It makes sense, therefore, to look for the identity of those referred to cryptically – like the Teacher of Righteousness and the Wicked Priest – within the same earlier period.

Finally, Thiering's supposed emulation of 1QpHab's use of the Bible in her own reading of the Gospels is thoroughly misleading. A document like 1QpHab is often, quite reasonably, dubbed a Pesher or Commentary by scholars, because it follows each biblical citation with an interpretation introduced by the Hebrew word *pesher* ('interpretation'). Persons and events mentioned in the former are reapplied imaginatively to the time of the author in the latter, as we noted earlier.[30] However, the writers of 1QpHab or 4QpNah spell out their interpretations of the scriptural text quite straightforwardly; they did not intend their own compositions to be treated as cryptic works in turn by future generations. The same point applies to the Gospels. They too claim various Old Testament passages have found their fulfilment in the ministry of Jesus. But we have absolutely no evidence whatsoever to suggest that the writers shaped their accounts so as to conceal under the surface additional data which only Thiering has been able to decipher. In reality, she has cast her own projections into the void created by her fanciful rejection of a more sober account of the sectarian DSS. The cumulative evidence shows her conclusions are nonsense.

THE FASCINATION OF THE DEAD SEA SCROLLS

Sensationalist speculation about the significance of the DSS did not begin with the musings of Baigent and Leigh, Thiering and others, for, ever since their discovery, these remarkable documents from the Judaean desert have been subjected to outlandish interpretations.

When it comes to Eisenman's hypothesis and the conspiracy theory of Baigent and Leigh, indeed, many of their ideas replicate those put forward in the 1950s and 1960s by the critic Edmund Wilson and the sometime scholar John Allegro. Thus, Wilson wrote an article for the *New Yorker* in 1955 and subsequently published a book later in the same year entitled *The Scrolls from the Dead Sea*.[31] Popularizing the more circumspect views of the French scholar, Andre Dupont-Sommer of the Sorbonne University, Wilson maintained that the small team of Qumran scholars in control of the texts was withholding information which proved that the DSS contained beliefs which hitherto had been thought uniquely Christian.[32] There is, of course, a grain of truth in this, for, on the basis of the DSS and other Second Temple evidence, we learned in the previous chapter just how Jewish Jesus and the early Christians were. But Wilson had more sensational links in mind, such as belief in the death and resurrection of the Messiah. To date, as will be clear already, no such documents have come to light, even after the release of outstanding Cave 4 material in 1991.

John M. Allegro, one of the small band of original Qumran scholars, made similar statements in three lectures given on British radio in 1956. He alleged that the DSS contained references to Christian doctrines – including a messianic crucifixion and resurrection – which would be damaging to the Church if revealed to the public. Even though the other members of the team publicly denied his claim, Allegro elaborated ever more fanciful theories about the DSS and their relation to Christianity.[33] Ultimately, he destroyed his academic credibility with the publication of his infamous book *The Sacred Mushroom and the Cross*, a fantasy which maintains that the Christian tradition stems back to the hallucinogenic effects of certain mushrooms![34]

As for his claim that some DSS contained references to crucifixion and other 'Christian' ideas, Allegro must have had in mind the two damaged documents considered in the previous section – 4QRule of War and 4QarApocal – and, presumably, 4QMessApoc. Now that all the manuscripts and fragments are freely available, nothing else has come to light which could be construed in such a way. Even so, although these three works do mention someone's death, a 'son of God', and resurrection, respectively, our earlier discussion showed that it would be a grave error to interpret them along the lines of Allegro, Wilson or, more recently, Eisenman. With the benefit of hindsight, therefore, it is no wonder that relations between Allegro and his fellow team members deteriorated. On the other hand, if the material concerned had been published fully at the time, the energy expended on recurrently sensationalizing the subject could have been redirected to more rewarding endeavour.

Yet, maybe there is some deeper element in the human psyche which is driven to mystify such matters. Even back in 1910, with the publication of the copy of the Damascus

Document found in Cairo in 1897, the *New York Times* ran a Christmas Day headline claiming that the manuscripts concerned described 'personages believed to be Christ, John the Baptist, and the Apostle Paul'![35] This announcement followed the publication of the document, but, it ought to be made clear, did not reflect the views of the man who knew most about it, the renowned Cambridge scholar Solomon Schechter.[36] It did receive support from George Margoliouth of the British Museum, however, who was of the opinion that the Damascus Document's 'Messiah of Aaron' was none other than John the Baptist, while the Teacher of Righteousness was Jesus and the Scoffer was Paul. Since then, as we have seen, the media have lapped up similar reports, with the help of the occasional renegade scholar.

Surely there is a rational explanation for this apparently limitless propensity to link the DSS with Jesus and Christianity in what, certainly after almost fifty years of Qumran research, is rather a credulous manner? Part of the answer lies in the fact that the Christian religion in its various forms has saturated the culture of Western Europe and North America for hundreds of years, coupled with traditional views of the Bible, Jesus, Judaism and Christianity itself. Accordingly, most people throughout the centuries have assumed, and still assume, that Jesus and the early Christians were the most important players in the world of their time. Even with the rise of academic study of the Bible and of Jewish and Christian history, many scholars found it difficult to put on hold pervasive assumptions derived from the dominance of Christianity through the centuries. For example, late nineteenth and early twentieth century studies of Judaism in the time of Jesus were often tinged, albeit subtly, with traditional Christian caricatures of Jewish religion that derived from the polemics of a previous age.[37]

Fortunately, scholars working today are much more aware of the potential presuppositions have for affecting the way they approach their subject matter. This does not mean that they need stop being Jewish or Christian or of any other persuasion. However, the realization of the danger is half the battle, for it allows a person's preconceptions to be acknowledged, held in check or overridden, as appropriate. The rise of liberal versions of Judaism and Christianity has also helped. Although the adherents of these forms of Jewish and Christian religion remain a minority, their existence has provided forms of religious expression which have been able to absorb the results of historical scholarship, even when they conflict with a more traditional religious outlook.

Most non-specialists, it has to be said, remain unaware of such developments. This applies both to those who are religious and to those who are not. The latter, indeed, just like everyone else, tend to pick up a picture of Judaism or Christianity derived from the days before historical research on the Bible, Judaism and Christianity encouraged a more complex and less black-and-white understanding. Of course, when knowledge in every area of both the sciences and the arts is continually growing, it is not surprising to find that the results of academic study in this particular field are not widely appreciated. The reticence of many professional academics to explain their work to a general audience only makes things worse.

It also means that journalists – even when trying their best to be neutral and objective – can often be unaware of the uncritical, not to say traditional, framework within which they sporadically operate when it comes to matters of religion. An article in the *Independent* newspaper in September 1992, for example, was headed 'Scroll Fragment Challenges Basic Tenet of Christianity'. Despite the title, its discussion of 4QarApocal, a fragmentary text considered earlier in this chapter, quite sensibly stated that the reference to a 'son of God' probably denoted some divine pretender who would rule over the last empire on earth before the advent of God's kingdom. Mixed in with such sober judgement, however, and without really explaining why, it was also suggested that 4QarApocal might challenge 'the fundamental Christian belief that Jesus was the unique Son of God'.[38] It does nothing of the sort, of course, for the phrase would not have meant God the Son (that is, the Second Person of the Trinity), as the article's words imply at this point, to either Jews or Christians before 70 CE. Historical research into Second Temple Judaism and early Christianity has shown that this Christian belief only emerged in embryonic form towards the end of the first century CE as Jews and Christians parted company.

In shedding considerable, albeit indirect, light on early Christianity, study of the sectarian DSS has played a vital role in helping scholars come to such conclusions. We saw, for example, that it was the Christian movement's detachment from the Law which underlay the break between Judaism and Christianity in the final decades of the first century CE – not belief in the special role of Jesus in and of itself. Furthermore, the early Christian movement was originally one of several parties within Second Temple Judaism. Although scholars might eventually have arrived at a similar conclusion without the aid of the DSS, the Qumran documents have provided us with a clear testimony on this point: they too reflect a religious community which, although at a different time and in a different way, married devotion to the central core of common Judaism with an attachment to a religious leader who was rejected by others.

Most remarkably of all, the DSS have allowed the sort of direct access to the practices and beliefs of an Essene community which had not previously been thought imaginable. As the only first-hand evidence that has come to light about a religious party which flourished in Second Temple times, we have learned much about the group's origins and character and have also been able to catch a glimpse of its attitude towards

Jews outside. By combining the evidence of the DSS with other literature from the period, Second Temple Judaism now seems infinitely more complex and varied than scholars envisaged even a few decades ago. Moreover, this richness impacts on the nature of the Old Testament itself, for the luxury afforded by the recovery of biblical manuscripts from the Qumran caves has revealed a hitherto undreamed of fluidity in both the text and contents of the Bible.

Scholars are still reeling in response to the vast array of ancient documents they now have at their disposal, especially after the release of fresh DSS material in late 1991. Although, as we learned earlier, the publication of outstanding texts now proceeds apace, it will take some time to analyse these new compositions in depth and relate them more precisely to those that have been in the public domain much longer. In the decades to come, therefore, we can look forward to the emergence of an ever more subtle understanding of the Essene community at Qumran and its relationship with outsiders, as well as further insights into the nature of Second Temple Judaism as a whole in relation to what preceded in biblical times and what followed in the Rabbinic period.

Meanwhile, if this book about the DSS succeeds in disseminating more widely just how radically the fruits of academic study of the Bible, Judaism and Christianity can shape an informed view of the past, it will achieve its aim.

NOTES

1 *What Are the Dead Sea Scrolls?*

1 See Map 2.
2 For convenience, we shall employ 'Palestine' as equivalent to the vague 'Holy Land', including Judaea, Samaria, Galilee, Peraea and Idumaea. Historically, however, the name comes from the Latin *Palaestina* and in Roman times was used, with qualifying terms, to designate differing overlapping regions at different times.
3 J. C. Trever, *The Untold Story of Qumran*, New Jersey (1965), gives more detail than is possible here, as does his *The Dead Sea Scrolls: a Personal Account*, Grand Rapids (1977). See also M. Burrows, *The Dead Sea Scrolls*, New York (1955).
4 In the Syrian Orthodox Church, a Metropolitan is a kind of archbishop.
5 M. Burrows, J. C. Trever, W. H. Brownlee, *The Dead Sea Scrolls of St Mark's Monastery*, I–II, New Haven (1950–1).

6 After some perseverance, the work was unrolled and subsequently published in N. Avigad, Y. Yadin, *A Genesis Apocryphon*, Jerusalem (1956).
7 The codex – the form of the modern book – became popular with Christians from the second century CE and more widely from the fourth century CE. Jews to this day, though, continue to retain the scroll form for the liturgical use of sacred texts in the synagogue.
8 E. L. Sukenik, *The Dead Sea Scrolls of the Hebrew University*, Jerusalem (1954–5).
9 The Shrine was able to include even the Metropolitan's scrolls, for, after taking them to America in 1949 for safekeeping and then offering them for sale in the *Wall Street Journal*, in 1954 he unwittingly sold them back to Israel through a middleman for $250,000.
10 The news was further broadcast by W. F. Albright in the *Bulletin of the American Schools of Oriental*

Research 110 (April 1948), p. 3.

11 D. Barthelemy, J. T. Milik,
Discoveries in the Judaean Desert I:
Qumran Cave 1, Oxford (1955).

12 CE (Common Era) and BCE
(Before the Common Era) are
used throughout the book in
preference to AD and BC,
although they refer to the same
periods of time.

13 See Map 3.

14 The best detailed report of the
archaeological excavations is
still R. de Vaux, *Archaeology and*
the Dead Sea Scrolls, Oxford
(1973).

15 See J. A. Sanders, *Discoveries in*
the Judaean Desert of Jordan IV:
The Psalms Scroll of Qumran Cave
11, Oxford (1965), as well as
J. P. M. van der Ploeg, A. S. van
der Woude, B. Jongeling, *Le*
Targum de Job de la grotte XI de
Qumran, Leiden (1971) and D. N.
Freedman, K. A. Matthews, *The*
Paleo-Hebrew Leviticus Scroll
(11QpaleoLev), Winona Lake
(1985).

16 His impressive study of the
document was published in
Hebrew in 1977 and then in
English translation as *The Temple*
Scroll, I–III, Jerusalem (1983).

17 The First Revolt against Rome
(66–70 CE) and the Second
Revolt against Rome (132–
134 CE), as well as the much
earlier Maccabean Revolt (mid-
160s BCE), should be carefully

distinguished. All three will be
discussed more fully in Chapter 3.

18 In this sort of usage,
'apocryphon' can denote any
scripture-like book which failed
to enter the Bible. The
designation Apocrypha, the
plural form of apocryphon, will
be explained more fully below.

19 See Appendix I, which lists the
most important DSS from each
cave.

20 No works from the New
Testament were found in the
caves at all, despite claims to the
contrary. The implications of
this absence will be picked up in
Chapter 5.

21 The Damascus Document is the
only exception to note, for it had
already turned up some fifty
years earlier in a different edition
in an old synagogue in Cairo.
This important work will be
discussed further in Chapter 3.

22 He wrote a string of articles in
the *Jewish Quarterly Review* (of
which he was editor), beginning
with 'Scholarship and the Hoax
of Recent Discoveries', *Jewish*
Quarterly Review 39 (1949),
pp. 337–63.

23 The first six chapters of H.
Shanks (ed.), *Ancient Israel: A*
Short History from Abraham to the
Roman Destruction of the Temple,
London (1989), offer a good
outline of biblical history from
an academic viewpoint.

24 The First Temple, as it is called by historians, was completed about 927 BCE but destroyed by the Babylonians in 587 BCE.

25 The whole incident is recounted in detail by the ancient Jewish author Philo in his *On the Embassy to Gaius*, 31–42.

26 M. Baillet, J. T. Milik, R. de Vaux, *Discoveries in the Judaean Desert of Jordan III: Les Petites Grottes de Qumran*, Oxford (1962).

27 G. Vermes, *The Dead Sea Scrolls: Qumran in Perspective*, London (1977), p. 23f.

28 See J. M. Allegro, A. A. Anderson, *Discoveries in the Judaean Desert of Jordan V: Qumran Cave 4, I (4Q158– 4Q186)*, Oxford (1968), and the critical 114-page review by J. Strugnell, 'Notes en marge du Volume V des *Discoveries in the Judaean Desert of Jordan*', *Revue de Qumran* (1969–71), pp. 163– 276. The next volume was R. de Vaux, J. T. Milik, *Discoveries in the Judaean Desert VI: Qumran Grotte 4 II: I Archeologie; II Tefillin, Mezuzot et Targum (4Q128– 4Q157)*, Oxford (1977).

29 A third volume of Cave 4 texts, however, did appear while he was overall editor-in-chief: M. Baillet, *Discoveries in the Judaean Desert VII: Qumran Grotte 4: III (4Q482–4Q520)*, Oxford (1982).

30 This incident is recounted in the latest edition of Vermes' *The Dead Sea Scrolls: Qumran in Perspective*, London (1994), p. 8; the present author, one of his postgraduate students at the time, also attended the conference. To be fair, a collection of non-Qumran material was prepared while Strugnell was editor-in-chief: E. Tov (ed.), *Discoveries in the Judaean Desert VIII: The Greek Minor Prophets Scrolls from Nahal Hever (8HevXIIgr)*, Oxford (1990).

31 The story appeared in *Ha-aretz*, on 9 November 1990. An English version of the article can be read in H. Shanks (ed.), *Understanding the Dead Sea Scrolls*, London (1993), pp. 260– 63. Among other things, Strugnell described Judaism as a 'horrible religion'.

32 B. Z. Wacholder, M. Abegg, *A Preliminary Edition of the Unpublished Dead Sea Scrolls: the Hebrew and Aramaic Texts from Cave 4*, fascicle 1, Washington (1991).

33 R. H. Eisenman, J. M. Robinson, *A Facsimile Edition of the Dead Sea Scrolls*, I–II, Washington (1991).

34 See P. W. Skehan, E. Ulrich, J. E. Sanderson, *Discoveries in the Judaean Desert IX: Qumran Cave 4: IV: Paleo-Hebrew and Greek Biblical Manuscripts*, Oxford (1992); E. Qimron, J. Strugnell,

Discoveries in the Judaean Desert X: Qumran Cave 4: V: Miqsat Ma'ase ha-Torah, Oxford (1994); E. Ulrich, F. M. Cross, *Discoveries in the Judaean Desert XII: Qumran Cave 4: VII: Genesis to Numbers*, Oxford (1994); H. Attridge and others, *Discoveries in the Judaean Desert XIII: Qumran Cave 4: VIII: Parabiblical Texts – Part 1*, Oxford (1994); M. Broshi and others, *Discoveries in the Judaean Desert XIX: Qumran Cave 4: XIV: Parabiblical Texts – Part 2*, Oxford (1995).

35 See Map 2. Wadi is an Arabic term for a river bed which fills up with water only when it rains; Nahal is the equivalent word in Hebrew.

36 A good summary article on Wadi ed-Daliyeh can be found in D. N. Freedman (ed.), *The Anchor Bible Dictionary*, New York (1992).

37 On the Masada excavations, see Y. Yadin, *Masada: Herod's Fortress and the Zealots' Last Stand*, London (1966).

38 See J. T. Milik, R. de Vaux, *Discoveries in the Judaean Desert II: Les grottes de Murabba'at*, Oxford (1961), as well as E. Tov (ed.), *Discoveries in the Judaean Desert VIII: The Greek Minor Prophets Scrolls from Nahal Hever (8HevXIIgr)*, Oxford (1990).

39 The results of palaeographical analysis of the DSS will be considered more fully in Chapter 3.

2 The Dead Sea Scrolls and the Bible

1 A prime example was the work of James Moffat. He published *The New Testament: A New Translation* in 1913 and his Old Testament appeared in 1924; a revision of Moffat's Bible came out in 1935.

2 For examples, as well as a fuller history of the English Bible, see 'Translations' in B. M. Metzger, M. D. Coogan, *The Oxford Companion to the Bible*, Oxford (1993).

3 The divergence at the start of the verse, however, is purely stylistic. Although the Hebrew text reads 'The angel of the LORD' (NRSV), the REB has a shorter reference to 'The angel' simply because this figure was already mentioned as 'the angel of the LORD' in the preceding verse.

4 For an overview of academic study of the New Testament, see S. Brown, *The Origins of Christianity: A Historical Introduction to the New Testament*, Oxford (1993).

5 H. Shanks (ed.), *Ancient Israel: A Short History from Abraham to the Roman Destruction of the Temple*, London (1989), provides an

introduction to some of these matters.

6 Further discussion on individual biblical books can be found in A. J. Soggin, *Introduction to the Old Testament*, London (1989).

7 Daniel is the youngest book of all, completed in the 160s BCE several centuries after Daniel was supposed to have lived, as details in Daniel 11 show.

8 For more specific examples, see A. J. Soggin, *Introduction to the Old Testament*, London (1989), pp. 92–95.

9 Cyrus, the king of Persia who first allowed the exiles to return to Judah in 537 BCE, is mentioned by name in Isaiah 44:28 and 45:1–8.

10 One unconvincing attempt to reassert traditional dates of authorship can be found in E. J. Young, *Introduction to the Old Testament*, London (1960).

11 It should be noted, in addition, that some secondary versions, prepared on the basis of the Masoretic Text or the Septuagint, have long been in circulation. Latin translations, for example, were made by Christians in the first few centuries CE, the most famous being the Vulgate of St Jerome (342–420 CE). As for the Jews, they produced an Aramaic paraphrase of every book of the Hebrew Bible during the same period; these are known as the Targums or Targumim (singular, Targum).

12 The following illustration may clarify what is involved. Until recently, a leading British supermarket chain employed abbreviated forms of its products' names on some external packaging. Often, this would result in the description of an item without vowels. For example, one was labelled 'vrtlly ft fr mlk'. Surprisingly perhaps, this short version of 'virtually fat free milk' is instantly recognizable, especially for staff and customers familiar with the store's products. It so happens that Hebrew and Aramaic operate like this all the time when used as living languages.

13 A special scholarly edition of the Leningrad Codex now exists for academic use in the form of K. Elliger, W. Rudolph, *Biblia Hebraica Stuttgartensia*, Stuttgart (1967–83). This hefty tome includes in extensive footnotes variant readings from the LXX, the Samaritan Pentateuch and other versions, as compiled by modern scholars.

14 A translation of the Letter of Aristeas can be found in J. H. Charlesworth, *Old Testament Pseudepigrapha*, II (1983–85), pp. 7–34.

15 The most easily accessible edition of the Greek of the LXX

is A. Rahlfs, *Septuaginta*, Stuttgart (1979).

16 The text can be consulted in A. F. Gall, *Der Hebraische Pentateuch der Samaritaner*, I–IV, Giessen (1914–18); reprinted Berlin (1966).

17 More information on the interrelation of the Masoretic Text, Septuagint, and Samaritan Pentateuch can be found in the relevant entries in D. N. Freedman (ed.), *The Anchor Bible Dictionary*, New York (1992).

18 The clearest example of such bias can be seen in the Ten Commandments listed in Exodus 20 and Deuteronomy 5. The Samaritan Pentateuch has made the building of an altar on Mount Gerizim one of the commandments, clearly intending to assert this site, rather than Jerusalem, as the true holy place chosen by God.

19 Beginning with the left-hand column, the books are listed according to their traditional order in the Jewish Bible.

20 For discussion on the biblical DSS more detailed than what follows, see E. Tov, *Textual Criticism of the Hebrew Bible*, Minneapolis (1992).

21 See his *Jewish Antiquities*, 6.68–71.

22 For further discussion, see G. Vermes, 'The Dead Sea Scrolls

Forty Years On', *The Thirteenth Sacks Lecture*, Oxford (1987).

23 In Jewish circles, the acronym Tanakh – T(orah)aN(evi'im)aK(etuvim)h – is another way of referring to the scriptures.

24 Indeed, an English translation of the whole collection just listed is easily accessible in editions of the NRSV containing the Apocrypha/Deutero-canonical books.

25 The title 'Deutero-canonical' implies that the books concerned form a secondary layer of authoritative scripture which is, nonetheless, on a par with the rest of the Bible from the viewpoint of the Church authorities.

26 To clarify matters further, apart from the divergent manner in which the same Old Testament books are ordered, the only difference between Jewish and Protestant Bibles is the presence or absence of the New Testament.

27 As discussed earlier in this chapter, experts have also come to realize that the same feature applies to many books in the Old Testament, Apocrypha and New Testament.

28 A translation of these and other Pseudepigrapha is readily available in H. F. D. Sparks' inappropriately named *The

Apocryphal Old Testament, Oxford (1984). An even larger collection can be found in J. H. Charlesworth (ed.), *Old Testament Pseudepigrapha*, I–II, London (1983, 1985).

29 An English translation of the remains of copies of both documents can be found in F. García Martínez, *The Dead Sea Scrolls Translated*, Leiden (1994), pp. 238–59.

30 It ought to be pointed out that both G. Vermes, *The Dead Sea Scrolls in English*, London (1995), and F. García Martínez, *The Dead Sea Scrolls Translated*, Leiden (1994), contain translations of numerous DSS which belong to this second class and are not, strictly speaking, sectarian. See, for example, the so-called Testaments of Qahat (Moses' grandfather) and Amram (Moses' father).

31 For a full exposition of this position, see J. Barton, *Oracles of God*, London (1986), pp. 1–96.

32 Such a designation appears in Romans 3:21, for instance, where the Apostle Paul states that his argument is 'attested by the law and the prophets'.

33 The caves yielded the remains of some thirty-six copies of the Psalms, while the surviving portions of 4QpPs comment on Psalms 37, 45, 127 in much the same way that 1QpHab treats the text of Habakkuk 1–2.

34 In addition, CD 4:13 seems to refer to an earlier form of part of the Testament of the Twelve Patriarchs.

3 *Who Wrote the Dead Sea Scrolls?*

1 For the original report, see O. R. Sellars, 'Radiocarbon Dating of the Cloth from the "Ain Feshkha Cave"', *Bulletin of the American Schools of Oriental Research* 123 (1951), pp. 24–26.

2 See G. Bonani and others, 'Radiocarbon Dating of Fourteen Dead Sea Scrolls', *Radiocarbon* 34 (1992), pp. 843–49.

3 See A. J. T. Jull and others, 'Radiocarbon Dating of Scrolls and Linen Fragments from the Judean Desert', *Radiocarbon* 37 (1995), p. 14.

4 The Nash Papyrus, a first-century CE Egyptian fragment containing the Ten Commandments from Deuteronomy 5, was the oldest known piece of Hebrew text before the DSS were found.

5 See Map 2.

6 The classic discussion of the palaeography of the DSS is still F. M. Cross, 'The Development of the Jewish Scripts', in *The Bible and the Ancient Near East:*

Essays in Honour of William Foxwell Albright, New York (1965), pp. 170–264.

7 A final report on the archaeological excavations is only now under way. Meanwhile, see R. de Vaux, *Archaeology and the Dead Sea Scrolls*, London (1973), or, for a lighter introduction, P. R. Davies, *Qumran*, Grand Rapids (1983).

8 Josephus mentions this earthquake in his *Jewish Antiquities*, 15.121.

9 See Map 4.

10 For more detail, see the last two chapters of H. Shanks (ed.), *Ancient Israel: A Short History from Abraham to the Roman Destruction of the Temple*, London (1989).

11 See Map 1.

12 This event is still celebrated by Jews today in the festival of Hanukkah (Re-dedication).

13 See 1 Kings 4:25 and Micah 4:4.

14 The name comes from Hasmon, Judah's great-great-grandfather.

15 See Map 5.

16 Reports of this aggressive Judaization probably fuelled the negative picture of Judaism that gained currency among many Gentile writers soon afterwards. The first-century BCE classical author Cicero, for example, described Judaism as a 'barbarous superstition'.

17 *Jewish Antiquities*, 13.372.

18 *Jewish Antiquities*, 13.380–83.

19 Unless otherwise stated, all citations from the sectarian DSS are according to G. Vermes, *The Dead Sea Scrolls in English*, London (1995). It should be pointed out that square brackets in the translation of the scrolls by Vermes and others usually denote that the words within them constitute a reconstruction of damaged parts of a given document; words in normal brackets merely supply supplementary data to communicate the original text's meaning.

20 Josephus goes into Herod's reign in some detail in *Jewish War*, 1 and *Jewish Antiquities*, 15–17.

21 See again Map 5.

22 See Mark 15:1.

23 Josephus has a very moving, if imaginative, account of their fate in *Jewish War*, 7.252–388.

24 The relevant passages from both writers, too numerous to list, can be found in G. Vermes, M. Goodman, *The Essenes According to the Classical Sources*, Sheffield (1989).

25 See *Jewish Antiquities*, 13.171–72.

26 See *Jewish War*, 2.122.

27 See *Jewish War*, 2.129–31.

28 See *Jewish War*, 2.160–61.

29 See *Natural History*, 5.73.

30 See the Damascus Document, 7:6–9.

31 Josephus makes this assertion in his *Life*, 10–12.

32 Even Pliny has a tendency to present his account as 'tourist information' for his Latin readers – Qumran residents would, in reality, have had to travel to Jericho or En Gedi to view palm trees.

33 For a fuller survey, see G. Vermes, *The Dead Sea Scrolls: Qumran in Perspective*, London (1994), pp. 58–72.

34 This rendering is the author's own, based on the Hebrew composite text of 4QMMT in E. Qimron, J. Strugnell, *Discoveries in the Judaean Desert X: Qumran Cave 4: V: Miqsat Ma'ase ha-Torah*, Oxford (1994), p. 62.

35 See E. Qimron, J. Strugnell, *Discoveries in the Judaean Desert X: Qumran Cave 4: V: Miqsat Ma'ase ha-Torah*, Oxford (1994).

36 1QS 4:25, however, implies that some kind of 'renewal' or metamorphosis will follow.

37 For a variety of views on 11QT, see G. J. Brooke (ed.), *Temple Scroll Studies*, Sheffield (1989). Some maintain that links with CD are not strong enough to count 11QT among the sectarian DSS; in that case, it belongs to the second category of material described in Chapter 1.

38 For the sake of clarity in the parallelism, the translation of 11QT 56:12–18 is the author's own, but mirrors the NRSV as far as possible.

39 A preliminary translation can be found in R. Eisenman, M. Wise, *The Dead Sea Scrolls Uncovered*, London (1992), pp. 125–27.

40 See A. J. T. Jull and others, 'Radiocarbon Dating of Scrolls and Linen Fragments from the Judean Desert', *Radiocarbon* 37 (1995), p. 14.

41 The following translation by Vermes appears with the numbers of the lines added in order to aid subsequent discussion.

42 H. Stegemann has proposed that the Teacher of Righteousness was the High Priest deposed by Jonathan Maccabee in 152 BCE, although he has not been followed by most scholars. Most recently, see his lengthy article 'The Qumran Essenes – Local Members of the Main Jewish Union in Late Second Temple Times', in J. T. Barrera, L. V. Montaner, *The Madrid Qumran Congress: Proceedings of the International Congress on the Dead Sea Scrolls Madrid 18–21 March, 1991*, I, Leiden (1992), pp. 83–166.

43 For an exposition of the relevant passages, see the useful commentary accompanying the translation of the text of 1QpHab in M. Knibb, *The Qumran Community*, Cambridge (1987), pp. 221–46.

44 See above, p. 68.

45 The number of documents retrieved from Cave 4 and the poor condition of many of them have led some to suggest that the site was a *geniza* – a place for discarding worn-out sacred texts instead of destroying them – during all or part of the sect's two hundred-year occupation of Qumran.

46 A fuller account is easily accessible in G. Vermes, *The Dead Sea Scrolls: Qumran in Perspective*, London (1994).

47 P. R. Davies, *The Damascus Covenant*, Sheffield (1982).

48 F. Garcia Martinez, A. S. van der Woude, 'Qumran Origins and Early History: a Groningen Hypothesis', *Revue de Qumran* (1990), pp. 521–42.

49 A similar combination is to be found in the Testament of the Twelve Patriarchs, another pseudepigraphical work from the Second Temple period, the precise date of which is difficult to determine in view of later Christian interpolations.

50 A number of scholars have suggested that the sect believed this messianic prophet to have arrived already in the form of the Teacher of Righteousness himself. See, for example, G. Vermes, *The Dead Sea Scrolls: Qumran in Perspective*, London (1994), p. 170.

51 See Acts 5:17, and *Jewish Antiquities*, 13.296–98; 18.4; 20.199. For a fuller description, consult 'Sadducees' in D. N. Freedman, *The Anchor Bible Dictionary*, New York (1992).

52 One such attempt was that of R. North, 'The Qumran Sadducees', *Catholic Biblical Quarterly* 17 (1955), pp. 164–88.

53 More detail on the Pharisees can be found in D. N. Freedman, *The Anchor Bible Dictionary*, New York (1992).

54 One advocate of the identification of those at Qumran with the Pharisees was C. Rabin, *Qumran Studies*, Oxford (1957).

55 On the Zealots, see again D. N. Freedman, *The Anchor Bible Dictionary*, New York (1992). Alternatively, consult E. Schurer, G. Vermes and others, *The History of the Jewish People in the Age of Jesus Christ*, Edinburgh (1979), II, pp. 598–606.

56 This position was advanced by both C. Roth, *The Historical Background of the Dead Sea Scrolls*, Oxford (1958), and G. R. Driver, *The Judaean Scrolls: the Problem and a Solution*, Oxford (1965).

57 H. Stegemann has further proposed, for instance, that none of the Essenes were, in fact, celibate. See 'The Qumran Essenes – Local Members of the Main Jewish Union in Late Second Temple Times', in J. T.

Barrera, L. V. Montaner, *The Madrid Qumran Congress: Proceedings of the International Congress on the Dead Sea Scrolls Madrid 18–21 March, 1991*, I, Leiden (1992), pp. 83–166.

4 *The Dead Sea Scrolls and Judaism*

1 Henceforth, he called himself Flavius Josephus, prefixing his own name with the family name of the Flavian emperors Vespasian, Titus and Domitian.

2 We have already referred to the first three works. The *Life* is a short justification of Josephus' own role as a general in the First Revolt against Rome, while *Against Apion* is a defence of Judaism against the charges levelled by Apion and other anti-Jewish authors.

3 For an in-depth study of the man and his work, see T. Rajak, *Josephus: the Historian and His Society*, London (1983).

4 See, for example, J. Neusner, W. S. Green, E. S. Frerichs, *Judaisms and their Messiahs at the Turn of the Christian Era*, Cambridge (1987).

5 However, the suggestion that the Scribes formed another distinct community is likely to be incorrect. 'Scribe' was probably a loose designation for all sorts of literary functionaries, often

priests, who worked in an administrative capacity in the Jerusalem Temple and elsewhere. See, for example, Mark 2:15.

6 Although fictitiously ascribed to King Solomon of biblical times, Wisdom was penned in Greek in Egypt, probably around the time Philo himself was born.

7 Based on a variety of factors (like grain production, the size of inhabited areas, or figures given by Josephus), scholarly estimations of the size of the Jewish population in Second Temple times vary. See, for example, M. Broshi, 'Estimating the Population of Ancient Jerusalem', *Biblical Archaeological Review* 4 (1978), pp. 10–15. Overall, a figure of several million worldwide seems reasonable.

8 This has been argued by E. P. Sanders, *Judaism: Practice and Belief 63 BCE–66 CE*, London (1992).

9 Biblical instructions for the spring and summer festivals of Passover and Weeks, as well as the autumn convocations of Tabernacles and the Day of Atonement, are found in Exodus 23, Leviticus 16 and 23, and Deuteronomy 16.

10 See, for example, Matthew 17:24, as well as Philo's *On the Embassy to Gaius*, 156.

11 This humiliating decree was never officially revoked.

12 See, for example, the description of the Jews by the first- and second-century CE author Tacitus in his *Historiae*, V. 1–13.

13 Cassius Dio, *Roman History*, 37.16.2.

14 For the Sabbath and the prohibition against images, see Exodus 20:4–5, 8–11 and Deuteronomy 5:8, 12–15; the command to circumcise males is found in Genesis 17:12. For food laws, see Leviticus 11 and Deuteronomy 14, while some purity regulations are contained in Leviticus 15.

15 See *Jewish War*, 2.169–74.

16 *Jewish Antiquities*, 18.15, 17.

17 See, for example, his *Jewish Antiquities*, 18.16.

18 According to 1 Enoch 6–16 and Jubilees 10:1–14, the offspring of this illicit union took the form of demons which have plagued and victimized humanity ever since, bringing all manner of evil upon the earth; they will eventually be destroyed at the eschatological battle.

19 For an overview, see J. G. Campbell, 'Messianic Hope in Second Temple Judaism', in F. Bowie, C. Williams, *The Coming Redeemer*, Cardiff (forthcoming, 1997).

20 Portions of 1 Enoch, for example, look forward variously to an imminent vindication for the upright, a new heaven and earth, a new Jerusalem, the advent of a messianic figure, and a reversion to the primordial bliss of creation. See especially the so-called Animal Vision (1 Enoch 85–90) and the Apocalypse of Weeks (1 Enoch 91:11–17 and 93:1–10).

21 See above, p. 99.

22 In that case, the NRSV is wrong to use 'Rabbi' instead of 'master' in Mark 9:5 and 11:21.

23 This story is narrated in several Rabbinic sources, including the Babylonian Talmud in tractate Gittin, 59b.

24 Babylon took over as the centre of Jewish learning from the fourth century CE. This development explains why it was the Babylonian Talmud (*circa* 550 CE), rather than the shorter Palestinian Talmud (*circa* 450 CE), which gained the upper hand.

25 For more information, see 'Synagogue' in B. M Metzger, M. D. Coogan, *The Oxford Companion to the Bible*, Oxford (1993).

26 A number of useful introductions to the Mishnah and other important Rabbinic works, including the Talmud, are available. See, for example, H. Maccoby, *Early Rabbinic*

Writings, Cambridge (1990), as well as J. Neusner, *Invitation to the Talmud*, New York (1985), and *Invitation to Midrash*, New York (1991).

27 This citation is from H. Danby, *The Mishnah*, Oxford (1933), p. 446–47; a 'b.' in the text denotes the Hebrew word *ben*, meaning 'son of'.

28 This scriptural quotation is taken from Zechariah 8:16.

29 Rabbinic literature often refers to an individual legal decision as a *halakhah* (plural, *halakhot*), a Hebrew word derived from a verb 'to walk, to behave'. Consequently, the whole Rabbinic corpus of legal discussion can be referred to collectively as the Halakhah.

30 A fuller introduction to the Rabbinic idea of the Dual Torah can be found in J. Neusner, *Torah Through the Ages*, London (1990).

31 Such activity, as opposed to legal interpretation, is often referred to as *aggadah*, from a Hebrew verb 'to narrate'. Accordingly, the entire aggadic corpus can be called the Aggadah.

32 Further examples can be found in E. Schurer, G. Vermes and others, *The History of the Jewish People in the Age of Jesus Christ*, Edinburgh (1983), II, pp. 346–55.

33 The course of the Second Revolt against Rome is difficult to trace, due to the sparsity of ancient sources that mention it. See E. Schurer, G. Vermes and others, *The History of the Jewish People in the Age of Jesus Christ*, Edinburgh (1979), I, pp. 534–57, for more details.

34 The writings of Moses Maimonides (1135–1204) embody the height of Jewish medieval philosophy, especially his work entitled *Guide for the Perplexed*. As for Jewish mysticism, often called the Qabbalah from a Hebrew word meaning 'tradition', the Zohar (compiled *circa* 1200) was the main text produced in the Middle Ages. An overview of both can be found in D. Cohn-Sherbok, *The Jewish Heritage*, Oxford (1988).

35 On the origins and nature of Orthodox, Conservative and Reform Judaism, see N. de Lange, *Judaism*, Oxford (1986).

36 For fuller analyses from a variety of viewpoints, see D. Cohn-Sherbok, *The Future of Judaism*, Edinburgh (1994), J. Neusner, *Judaism in Modern Times: an Introduction and Reader*, Oxford (1995), and J. Sacks, *One People? Tradition, Modernity, and Jewish Unity*, London (1993).

37 See above, p. 54–55.

38 See above, p. 123–25.

39 For more on this and other issues as they affect Judaism in Britain,

see the author's chapter, 'The Jewish Community in Britain', in S. Gilley, W. J. Sheils (eds), *Religious Practice and Belief: A History of Religion in Britain*, Oxford (Blackwell, 1994), pp. 427–48.

5 *Christianity Reconsidered*

1 For an overview, see S. Brown, *The Origins of Christianity: A Historical Introduction to the New Testament*, Oxford (1993).

2 Individual books of the New Testament are discussed in detail by W. G. Kummel, *Introduction to the New Testament*, London (1975).

3 For further details, see R. Maddox, *The Purpose of Luke–Acts*, Edinburgh (1982).

4 Paul mentions a certain Luke as one of his 'fellow workers' in Philemon 24, while the pseudonymous Colossians 4:14 refers to 'Luke the beloved Physician'. Although Luke and Acts were probably composed by the same person, there is a modern scholarly consensus that the anonymous author actually worked around 90 CE.

5 On this theme, see J. Reumann, *Variety and Unity in New Testament Thought*, Oxford (1991).

6 J. N. D. Kelly, *2 Peter and Jude*, London (1969) is still a good commentary. It is widely held that 2 Peter, presented pseudonymously as the last testament of the Apostle Peter, was penned at the beginning of the second century CE.

7 Most of the books now in the New Testament were in general use among Christians from the late second century CE, although the oldest surviving fixed list which records them all dates to 367 CE. A collection of later Gospels and letters excluded from the New Testament canon, usually referred to as the New Testament Apocrypha, can be found in English translation in M. R. James, *The Apocryphal New Testament*, Oxford (1924).

8 A Jesuit priest called Jose O'Callaghan argued that the fragments 7Q3–18 were remnants of Mark, Acts, Romans, 1 Timothy, James and 2 Peter in 'Papiros neotestamentarios en la cueva 7 de Qumran?', *Biblica* 53 (1972), pp. 91–100; he was followed by C. P. Thiede, '7Q – Eine Ruckkehr zu den neutestamentlichen Papyrusfragmente in der siebten Hohle von Qumran', *Biblica* 65 (1984), pp. 528–59. A more sober judgement would describe 7Q3–18 as unidentifiable scraps, some of which might be the remains of Old Testament texts.

9 For more detail, see O. Betz, R.

Riesner, *Jesus, Qumran and the Vatican*, London (1994), pp. 114–24.

10 A. Schweitzer, *The Quest of the Historical Jesus*, London (1910), was an example of the former, while the latter is represented by the influential work of R. Bultmann, especially his *Theology of the New Testament*, I–II, London (1952, 1955).

11 Thus, see G. Vermes, *Jesus the Jew*, London (1973), and *The Religion of Jesus the Jew*, London (1993), as well as E. P. Sanders, *Jesus and Judaism*, London (1985).

12 Such a reconstruction requires us to discount the placing of Jesus' birth at the time of the census of 6 CE, as narrated in Luke 2:1–7.

13 More detailed discussion of the trial of Jesus can be found in D. Catchpole, *The Trial of Jesus*, Leiden (1971).

14 See *Jewish War*, 2.258–60, *Jewish Antiquities*, 20.97–98, and Acts 5:36.

15 Josephus boasts of his own reputation as a precocious fourteen-year-old in *Life*, 8. The motif is remarkably similar to that in Luke 2:41–52 and may have been a standard literary device.

16 Josephus, it should be pointed out, does give a resume of the careers of John the Baptist and Jesus in *Jewish Antiquities*, 18.62–64, 116–19. While the former is probably genuine, it is universally agreed that the latter was composed or expanded by a later Christian copyist. According to G. Vermes, 'The Jesus Notice of Josephus re-examined', *Journal of Jewish Studies* 38 (1987), pp. 1–10, Josephus' original words were:

> At about this time lived Jesus … He accomplished astonishing deeds … He won over many Jews … He was [called] Christ. When Pilate, upon the indictment brought by the principal men among us, condemned him to the cross, those who loved him from the very first did not cease to be attached to him … And the tribe of the Christians, so called after him, has to this day not disappeared.

17 By way of a reminder, we encountered named individuals in the sectarian DSS such as Antiochus IV, Demetrius III, Alexandra Salome and Aemilius Scaurus, while cryptic references included mention of the Teacher of Righteousness, the Wicked Priest and the Seekers of Smooth Things.

18 We observed in Chapter 2 that Greek became the common language of the churches once they had begun to flourish in the

Diaspora. Jews living in places like Egypt, of course, had already adopted Greek, and so a translation of the scriptures was available for Christian usage.

19 The remains of 1 Enoch at Qumran, as well as previously unknown works of a comparable nature, show that such speculation was rife among the sectarians and, because none of the documents seem to have been composed by the group, elsewhere. As we saw earlier, Jude 9 and 14–15 demonstrate that early Christians, too, were partial to drawing on such speculative traditions.

20 See above, p. 99.

21 See Hebrews 1:5 (citing Psalm 2:7 and 2 Samuel 7:14) and 4:14–16.

22 For further details, see B. Pixner, D. Chen, S. Margalit, 'Mount Zion: The Gate of the Essenes Re-excavated', *Zeitschrift des Deutschen-Palastina-Vereins* 105 (1989), pp. 85–95, as well as R. Riesner, 'Jesus, the Primitive Community and the Essene Quarter of Jerusalem', in J. H. Charlesworth (ed.), *Jesus and the Dead Sea Scrolls*, New York (1993).

23 See *Jewish War*, 5.145, and *Jewish Antiquities*, 15.373–79.

24 The title for this section has been borrowed from M. Casey, *From Jewish Prophet to Gentile God: the Origins and Development of New Testament Christology*, Cambridge (1991), whose ideas have had a considerable influence on what follows.

25 From the same period or later come other sayings in the Gospels and Acts, such as Mark 16:15 and Acts 1:8, in which Jesus commands a mission to the Gentiles.

26 Josephus testifies to the existence of such Gentile sympathizers at various points in his *Jewish Antiquities*, as do several passages in Acts (see Acts 13:26, for example, and 17:4).

27 For further discussion, see M. Casey, *From Jewish Prophet to Gentile God: the Origins and Development of New Testament Christology*, Cambridge (1991), J. D. G. Dunn, *Jesus, Paul and the Law*, London (1990), and J. T. Sanders, *Schismatics, Sectarians, Dissidents, Deviants: The First 100 Years of Jewish–Christian Relations*, London (1993).

28 For more details on the contents of such creeds and definitions, see the relevant entries in F. L. Cross, E. A. Livingstone, *The Oxford Dictionary of the Christian Church*, Oxford (1983).

29 To pursue this theme further, see the joint Jewish–Christian study by R. Rubinstein, J. K.

Roth, *Approaches to Auschwitz*, London (1987).

30 See, among other works, C. Rowland, *Christian Origins*, London (1985).

31 For more detailed discussion of some of these issues, see H. Küng, *On Being a Christian*, London (1977), and E. Schillebeeckx, *Christ: The Christian Experience in the Modern World*, London (1980).

6 Controversy and Conspiracy

1 See above, pp. 93–94.

2 See his 'The New Halakhic Letter (4QMMT) and the Origins of the Dead Sea Sect', *Biblical Archaeologist* 53 (1990), pp. 64–73; or 'The Sadducean Origins of the Dead Sea Scroll Sect', in H. Shanks (ed.), *Understanding the Dead Sea Scrolls*, London (1992), pp. 35–49.

3 This translation is taken from H. Danby, *The Mishnah*, Oxford (1933), p. 784.

4 This rendering is the author's own, based on the Hebrew composite text of 4QMMT in E. Qimron, J. Strugnell, *Discoveries in the Judaean Desert X: Qumran Cave 4: V: Miqsat Ma'ase ha-Torah*, Oxford (1994), p. 52.

5 See above, pp. 100–3. It is noteworthy that the writer of 4QMMT states elsewhere 'we separated from the multitude of

the people'. The Hebrew for 'we separated' is *parashnu*, a form of the verb *parash* from which the word Pharisee is commonly derived by scholars.

6 L. H. Schiffman, *Reclaiming the Dead Sea Scrolls: The History of Judaism, the Background of Christianity, and the Lost Library of Qumran*, Philadelphia (1994).

7 See N. Golb, 'The Problem of Origin and Identification of the Dead Sea Scrolls', *Proceedings of the American Philosophical Society* 124 (1980), pp. 1–24; 'Who Hid the Dead Sea Scrolls?', *Biblical Archaeologist* 28 (1987), pp. 68–82.

8 N. Golb, *Who Wrote the Dead Sea Scrolls?*, London (1995).

9 N. Golb, *Who Wrote the Dead Sea Scrolls?*, London (1995), p. 256–58.

10 See above, p. 90, as well as G. Vermes, *The Dead Sea Scrolls in English*, London (1995), p. 246.

11 See above, p. 87.

12 See again, N. Golb, *Who Wrote the Dead Sea Scrolls?*, London (1995), pp. 3–14.

13 For the research of P. Donceel-Voûte, see ' "Cenaculum" – La salle a l'etage du locus 30 a Khirbet Qumran sur la mer morte', *Res Orientales* 4 (1993), pp. 61–84.

14 See Map 3.

15 See R. Reich, 'A Note on the Function of Room 30 (the

"Scriptorium") at Khirbet Qumran', *Journal of Jewish Studies* XLVI (1995), pp. 157–60.

16 M. Baigent, R. Leigh, *The Dead Sea Scrolls Deception*, London (1991).

17 The German edition of the book was issued under the title *Verschlussache Jesus* – 'Classified Information on Jesus'.

18 Eisenman's main works are *Maccabees, Zadokites, Christians and Qumran*, Leiden (1983), and *James the Just in the Habakkuk Pesher*, Leiden (1986).

19 *Jewish Antiquities*, 20.200.

20 For this heartless action, it ought to be added, Josephus goes on to inform us that other more fair-minded Jews had Ananus deposed and replaced.

21 R. H. Eisenman, M. Wise, *The Dead Sea Scrolls Uncovered*, London (1992).

22 R. H. Eisenman, M. Wise, *The Dead Sea Scrolls Uncovered*, London (1992), p. 29.

23 See, for example, the article entitled 'Scrolls Question Messianic Theory' in *The Times*, 9 November 1991, p. 10.

24 See, for instance, R. H. Eisenman, M. Wise, *The Dead Sea Scrolls Uncovered*, London (1992), pp. 12–13, where palaeographical work and carbon dating are dismissed as unreliable in three short paragraphs.

25 Thus, see, J. A. Fitzmyer, 'The Contribution of Qumran Aramaic to the Study of the New Testament', *New Testament Studies* 20 (1974), pp. 382–401.

26 See, for example, her 'Qumran Initiation and New Testament Baptism', *New Testament Studies* 27 (1981), pp. 615–31, and 'The Date of Composition of the Temple Scroll', in G. J. Brooke (ed.), *Temple Scroll Studies*, Sheffield (1989), pp. 99–120.

27 B. Thiering, *Jesus the Man: A New Interpretation from the Dead Sea Scrolls*, London (1992). The same book appeared in North America under the title *Jesus and the Riddle of the Dead Sea Scrolls: Unlocking the Secrets of His Life Story*, San Francisco (1992).

28 See above, p. 90.

29 See above, pp. 57–59.

30 See above, pp. 83–84.

31 See E. Wilson, 'A Reporter at Large', *New Yorker*, 14 May 1955, as well as *The Scrolls from the Dead Sea*, New York (1955); the latter was subsequently expanded as *The Dead Sea Scrolls 1947–1969*, London (1969).

32 For Dupont-Sommer, see his *The Essene Writings from Qumran*, Oxford (1961).

33 See R. de Vaux and others, 'Letter concerning certain Broadcast Statements of Mr J. Allegro', *The Times*, 16 March 1956, p. 11.

34 J. M. Allegro, *The Sacred Mushroom and the Cross*, London (1970).

35 This report featured in the *New York Times*, 25 December 1910, p. 1, under the headline 'Jewish Manuscript Antedating Gospels'.

36 S. Schechter, *Documents of Jewish Sectaries: Fragments of a Zadokite Work*, Cambridge (1910).

37 See, for instance, G. Bornkamm, *Jesus von Nazareth*, Stuttgart (1956). This German work, translated into English as *Jesus of Nazareth* as late as 1960, reflects the common assumptions of much late nineteenth- and early twentieth-century scholarship. It maintains that, while Jesus grew up within the Jewish world of his time, spiritually he stood outside its narrow legalistic confines which represented a deterioration of the pure religion of Old Testament times.

38 See the *Independent*, 1 September 1992, p. 5. It ought to be added that this slip has been more than outweighed by many other consistently accurate articles on the DSS in the *Independent* over the years. See, for example, the recent report of renewed excavations in the Qumran region, 'Dead Sea scroll search reopens', on 19 December 1995, p. 11.

APPENDIX I

Important Dead Sea Scrolls

Acronym	Description	Number
CAVE 1		
1QIsa^a	Isaiah	(Not Applicable)
1QIsa^b	Isaiah	(Not Applicable)
1QapGen	Genesis Apocryphon	(Not Applicable)
1QS	Community Rule	(Not Applicable)
1QM	War Scroll	(Not Applicable)
1QpHab	Habakkuk Commentary	(Not Applicable)
IQpMic	Micah Commentary	IQ168
1QH	Hymns Scroll	(Not Applicable)
1QJub^{a-b}	Jubilees	1Q17–18
1QSa	Messianic Rule, originally appended to 1QS	1Q28a
1QSb	List of blessings, originally appended to 1QS	1Q28b
CAVE 2		
2QSir	Ecclesiasticus	2Q18
2QJub^{a-b}	Jubilees	2Q19–20
CAVE 3		
3QTreasure	Copper Scroll	3Q15

CAVE 4

4QExod^f	Exodus	4Q17
4QSam^a	1–2 Samuel	4Q51
4QSam^c	1–2 Samuel	4Q53
4QJer^{a–e}	Jeremiah	4Q70–72
4QpHos^{a–b}	Hosea Commentary	4Q166–167
4QpNah	Nahum Commentary	4Q169
4QpPs^{a–b}	Psalms Commentary	4Q171, 173
4QFlor	Florilegium or Midrash on the Last Days	4Q174
4QTest	Testimonia or Messianic Anthology	4Q175
4QTob^{a–e}	Tobit	4Q196–200
4QEn^{a–f}	1 Enoch	4Q201–202
4QTLevi	Testament of Levi	4Q213
4QJub^{a–h}	Jubilees	4Q216–224
4QarApocal	Aramaic Apocalypse	4Q246
4QS^{a–j}	Community Rule	4Q255–264
4QD^{a–h}	Damascus Document	4Q266–273
4QRule of War	Rule of War, missing end of 1QM/4QM	4Q285
4QBront	Brontologion	4Q318
4QCalendarC	Calendrical Document	4Q322–324
4QpapDoodles	Scribbles on Papyrus	4Q361
4QPentPara	Pentateuchal Paraphrase	4Q365
4QMMT^{a–f}	Miqsat Ma'ase ha-Torah	4Q394–399
4QSirShab^{a–h}	Shirot 'Olat ha-Shabbat	4Q400–407
4QapPs & Jon	Apocryphal Psalm and King Jonathan Text	4Q448
4QMessApoc	Messianic Apocalypse	4Q521

4QTQahat	Testament of Qahat	4Q542

CAVE 5

5QDeut	Deuteronomy	5Q1

CAVE 7

7QpapLXXEpJer	Letter of Jeremiah	7Q2
7QpapBibFrags	Unidentified Greek Biblical fragments on papyrus	7Q3–5
7QpapUnid	Unidentified fragments on papyrus	7Q6–18

CAVE 11

11QpalaeoLev	Leviticus written in Old Hebrew	11Q1
11QPs^a	Canonical and non-canonical Psalms Collection	11Q5
11QtgJob	Targum or Aramaic paraphrase of Job	11Q10
11QJub	Jubilees	11Q12
11QMelch	Melchizedek Document	11Q13
11QShirShab	Shirot 'Olat ha-Shabbat	11Q17
11QT^a	Temple Scroll	11Q19

APPENDIX II

Further Reading

1 ONE-VOLUME WORKS ON THE DSS AND THE ESSENES:

F. García Martínez, J. L. Barrera, *The People of the Dead Sea Scrolls*, Leiden (1995)

H. Shanks (ed.), *Understanding the Dead Sea Scrolls*, London (1992)

J. C. VanderKam, *The Dead Sea Scrolls Today*, London (1994)

G. Vermes, *The Dead Sea Scrolls: Qumran in Perspective*, London (1994)

2 ENGLISH TRANSLATIONS OF THE DSS:

R. Eisenman, M. Wise, *The Dead Sea Scrolls Uncovered*, London (1992)

F. García Martínez, *The Dead Sea Scrolls Translated*, Leiden (1994)

M. Knibb, *The Qumran Community*, Cambridge (1987)

G. Vermes, *The Dead Sea Scrolls in English*, London (1995)

3 TRANSLATIONS OF RELATED WORKS:

The Holy Bible: New Revised Standard Version, Oxford (1989)

F. H. Colson, M. Whitaker, *Philo*, I–X, Cambridge, Mass. (1929–43)

H. Danby, *The Mishnah*, Oxford (1933)

I. Epstein (ed.), *The Babylonian Talmud*, I–XXXV, London (1935–52)

H. F. D. Sparks, *The Apocryphal Old Testament*, Oxford (1984)

H. StJ. Thackery, R. Marcus, L. Feldman, *Josephus*, I–X, Cambridge, Mass. (1926–55)

4 THE DSS IN THEIR ORIGINAL HEBREW, ARAMAIC OR GREEK:

Discoveries in the Judaean Desert, I–XIII, XIX, Oxford (1955–95)
R. Eisenman, M. Wise, *The Dead Sea Scrolls Uncovered*, London (1992)
E. Lohse, *Die Texte aus Qumran*, Darmstadt (1971)

5 MAPS AND DIAGRAMS:

J. B. Pritchard (ed.), *The Times Atlas of the Bible*, London (1987)

6 MORE DETAILED STUDIES:

O. Betz, R. Riesner, *Jesus, Qumran and the Vatican*, London (1994)
G. J. Brooke (ed.), *Temple Scroll Studies*, Sheffield (1989)
G. J. Brooke (ed.), *New Qumran Texts and Studies*, Leiden (1995)
S. Brown, *The Origins of Christianity: A Historical Introduction to the New Testament*, Oxford (1993)
J. G. Campbell, *The Use of Scripture in the Damascus Document 1–8, 19–20*, Berlin (1995)
M. Casey, *From Jewish Prophet to Gentile God: the Origins and Development of New Testament Christology*, Cambridge (1991)
J. H. Charlesworth (ed.), *Jesus and the Dead Sea Scrolls*, New York (1990)
R. J. Coggins, *Introducing the Old Testament*, Oxford (1990)
D. Cohn-Sherbok, *The Future of Judaism*, Edinburgh (1994)
P. R. Davies, *Behind the Essenes: History and Ideology in the Dead Sea Scrolls*, Atlanta (1987)
P. R. Davies, *Sects and Scrolls: Essays on Qumran and Related Topics*, Atlanta (1996)
D. Dimant, U. Rappaport, *The Dead Sea Scrolls: Forty Years of Research*, Leiden (1992)
L. L. Grabbe, *Judaism from Cyrus to Hadrian*, London (1992)
J. Murphy-O'Connor, *Paul and Qumran*, New York (1990)
J. Neusner, *Torah Through the Ages*, London (1990)
E. Qimron, *The Hebrew of the Dead Sea Scrolls*, Atlanta (1986)

E. P. Sanders, *Judaism: Practice and Belief 63 BCE–66 CE*, London (1992)

E. Schurer, G. Vermes and others, *The History of the Jewish People in the Age of Jesus Christ*, I–III.2, Edinburgh (1973–87)

L. H. Schiffman, *Sectarian Law and the Dead Sea Scrolls*, Chicago (1983)

E. Schillebeeckx, *Christ: The Christian Experience in the Modern World*, London (1980)

H. Shanks (ed.), *Ancient Israel: a Short History from Abraham to the Roman Destruction of the Temple*, London (1989)

A. J. Soggin, *An Introduction to the Old Testament*, London (1989)

R. de Vaux, *Archaeology and the Dead Sea Scrolls*, Oxford (1973)

INDEX

See Appendix I for scrolls and acronyms arranged by cave.

OTHER ULYSSES PRESS TITLES

JESUS AND BUDDHA
The Parallel Sayings

Marcus Borg, Editor
Introduction by Jack Kornfield

The unexplained parallels between the sayings of Jesus and Buddha have puzzled historians for over a century. This book traces the life stories and beliefs of both, then presents a comprehensive collection of their remarkably similar teachings on facing pages. Featuring over one hundred parallels, *Jesus and Buddha* lets you explore the relationship between the West's predominant religion and many of the eternal truths upon which Eastern beliefs are based. Hardcover. $19.95.

FOUR FACES
A Journey in Search of Jesus the Divine, the Jew, the Rebel, the Sage

Mark Tully
Introduction by Thomas Moore

As the search for the historical Jesus leads ever further beyond the Bible, a new image of Jesus is emerging. In *Four Faces*, award-winning BBC journalist Mark Tully travels the globe to bring together the most current theories about Jesus. Drawing on ancient texts, modern archaeology and interviews with historians, theologians and holy men, Tully paints a multilayered portrait of Jesus. *Four Faces* invites the reader to rethink Jesus and his role for the third millennium. $15.00

THE LIFE OF MARY AND BIRTH OF JESUS
The Ancient Infancy Gospel of James

Ronald F. Hock

Of Mary's biography, the New Testament tells us little. Yet scenes from her life decorate churches around the world and are well known to her admirers. The source of these stories is a little-known manuscript that tells the entire story of Mary's life. Originally circulated among second-century Christians, this Gospel is now available again. Here is the complete text together with reproductions of the artworks that illustrate the influence of this Gospel on Christian art. Hardcover. $16.00.

4000 YEARS OF CHRISTMAS
A Gift From the Ages

Earl W. Count and Alice Lawson Count
Introduction by Dan Wakefield

Tracing myths and folklore from the Near East to northern Europe, *4000 Years of Christmas* reveals the surprising origins of our modern Christmas holiday. Here are Bronze Age Babylonians exchanging gifts, early Europeans hanging fir sprigs to renew life and Romans merrily celebrating "Saturnalia." With flowing narrative and decorative illustrations, *4000 Years of Christmas* embarks on a journey across cultures and millenia to reveal a celebration that is at the heart of all humanity. Hardcover. Two color throughout. $16.00.

THE LOST GOSPEL Q
The Original Sayings of Jesus

Marcus Borg, Editor
Introduction by Thomas Moore

Lost for two thousand years, the Gospel Q brings the reader closer to the historical figure of Jesus than ever before. The sayings within this book represent the very first Gospel. Here is the original Sermon on the Mount, the Lord's Prayer and Beatitudes. Reconstructed by biblical historians, Q provides a window into the world of ancient Christianity. *The Lost Gospel Q* presents Jesus' sayings in an easily accessible form designed to let all who are interested in his original teachings read them. Hardcover. Two color throughout. $15.00.

A BOY NAMED JESUS
How the Early Years Shaped His Life

Robert Aron
Introduction by Bishop John Shelby Spong

In this compelling account of the "missing years" of Jesus' youth, a distinguished historian explores the elements that would have shaped Jesus' life. He details the cultural and religious influences that a young Jewish boy would have experienced—life in a devout family, learning a trade and encounters with Roman soldiers. Then he recounts the young Jesus' evolving relationship with God, showing how a boy rooted in the Jewish tradition laid the foundation for an entirely new religion. $14.00.

To order these or other Ulysses Press books call 800-377-2542 or write to Ulysses Press, P.O. Box 3440, Berkeley, CA 94703-3440. There is no charge for shipping on retail orders. California residents must include sales tax. Allow two to three weeks for delivery.

ABOUT THE AUTHOR

Dr. Jonathan Campbell is a lecturer in Jewish Studies at the University of Bristol. He published his doctoral thesis on the Scrolls while studying at Oxford University.